Dogg's Hamlet,
Cahoot's Macbeth

Dogg's Hamlet, Cahoot's Macbeth

TOM STOPPARD

FABER AND FABER

LONDON   BOSTON

First published in 1979 by Inter-Action Inprint
This edition published in 1980
by Faber and Faber Limited
3 Queen Square London WC1N 3AU
Printed in Great Britain by
Latimer Trend & Company Ltd Plymouth
All rights reserved

© *1980 by Tom Stoppard*

All rights whatsoever in this play are strictly
reserved and professional applications for permission
to perform it, etc., must be made in advance, before
rehearsals begin, to Fraser and Dunlop (Scripts)
Ltd. of 91 Regent Street, London W1, and amateur
applications for permission to perform it, etc., must
be made in advance, before rehearsals begin, to
Samuel French Ltd. of 26 Southampton Street,
London WC2.

British Library Cataloguing in Publication Data

Stoppard, Tom
Dogg's Hamlet, Cahoot's Macbeth.
I. Title
II. Stoppard, Tom. Cahoot's Macbeth
822'.9'14   PR6069.T6D/

ISBN 0–571–11581–0
ISBN 0–571–11573–x Pbk

Dogg's Hamlet is dedicated to
Professor Dogg and The Dogg's Troupe
of Inter-Action

Cahoot's Macbeth is dedicated to
the Czechoslovakian playwright
Pavel Kohout

Preface

The comma that divides *Dogg's Hamlet, Cahoot's Macbeth* also serves to unite two plays which have common elements: the first is hardly a play at all without the second, which cannot be performed without the first.

Dogg's Hamlet is a conflation of two pieces written for Ed Berman and Inter-Action; namely *Dogg's Our Pet*, which opened the Almost Free Theatre in Soho in December 1971, and *The Dogg's Troupe 15-Minute Hamlet*, which was written (or rather edited) for performance on a double-decker bus.

Dogg's Hamlet derives from a section of Wittgenstein's philosophical investigations. Consider the following scene. A man is building a platform using pieces of wood of different shapes and sizes. These are thrown to him by a second man, one at a time, as they are called for. An observer notes that each time the first man shouts 'Plank!' he is thrown a long flat piece. Then he calls 'Slab!' and is thrown a piece of a different shape. This happens a few times. There is a call for 'Block!' and a third shape is thrown. Finally a call for 'Cube!' produces a fourth type of piece. An observer would probably conclude that the different words described different shapes and sizes of the material. But this is not the only possible interpretation. Suppose, for example, the thrower knows in advance which pieces the builder needs, and in what order. In such a case there would be no need for the builder to name the pieces he requires but only to indicate when he is ready for the next one. So the calls might translate thus:

Plank	= Ready	Block	= Next
Slab	= Okay	Cube	= Thank you

In such a case, the observer would have made a false assumption, but the fact that he on the one hand and the builders on the other are using two different languages need not be apparent to either party. Moreover, it would also be possible that the two builders do not share a language either; and if life for them consisted only of building platforms in this manner there would be no reason for them to discover that each was using a language unknown to the other. This happy state of affairs would of course continue only as long as, through sheer co-incidence, each man's utterance made sense (even if not the same sense) to the other.

The appeal to me consisted in the possibility of writing a play which had to teach the audience the language the play was written in. The present text is a modest attempt to do this: I think one might have gone much further.

Cahoot's Macbeth is dedicated to the Czechoslovakian playwright Pavel Kohout. During the last decade of 'normalization' which followed the fall of Dubcek, thousands of Czechoslovaks have been prevented from pursuing their careers. Among them are many writers and actors.

During a short visit to Prague in 1977 I met Kohout and Pavel Landovsky, a well-known actor who had been banned from working for years since falling foul of the authorities. (It was Landovsky who was driving the car on the fateful day in January 1977 when the police stopped him and his friends and seized the first known copies of the document that became known as Charter 77.) One evening Landovsky took me backstage at one of the theatres where he had done some of his best work. A performance was going on at the time and his sense of fierce frustration is difficult to describe.

A year later Kohout wrote to me: 'As you know, many Czech theatre-people are not allowed to work in the theatre during the last years. As one of them who cannot live without theatre I was searching for a possibility to do theatre in spite of circumstances. Now I am glad to tell you that in a few days, after eight weeks rehearsals—a Living-Room Theatre is opening, with nothing smaller but Macbeth.

'What is LRT? A call-group. Everybody, who wants to have Macbeth at home with two great and forbidden Czech actors, Pavel Landovsky and Vlasta Chramostova, can invite his friends and call us. Five people will come with one suitcase.

8

'Pavel Landovsky and Vlasta Chramostova are starring Macbeth and Lady, a well known and forbidden young singer Vlastimil Tresnak is singing Malcolm and making music, one young girl, who couldn't study the theatre-school, Tereza Kohoutova, by chance my daughter, is playing little parts and reading remarks; and the last man, that's me . . .! is reading and a little bit playing the rest of the roles, on behalf of his great colleague.

'I think, he wouldn't be worried about it, it functions and promises to be not only a solution of our situation but also an interesting theatre event. I adapted the play, of course, but I am sure it is nevertheless Macbeth!'

The letter was written in June, and in August there was a postscript: 'Macbeth is now performed in Prague flats.'

Cahoot's Macbeth was inspired by these events. However, Cahoot is not Kohout, and this necessarily over-truncated *Macbeth* is not supposed to be a fair representation of Kohout's elegant seventy-five minute version.

TOM STOPPARD
August 1980

Dogg's Hamlet

Characters

BAKER
ABEL
CHARLIE
EASY
DOGG
LADY
FOX MAJOR
MRS DOGG
SHAKESPEARE
HAMLET
HORATIO
CLAUDIUS
GERTRUDE
POLONIUS
OPHELIA
LAERTES
GHOST
BERNARDO
FRANCISCO
GRAVEDIGGER
OSRIC
FORTINBRAS

The first stage performance of *Dogg's Hamlet, Cahoot's Macbeth* was at the Arts Centre of the University of Warwick, Coventry, on 21 May 1979, by BARC, British American Repertory Company. The cast of BARC was:

John Challis
Alison Frazer
Ben Gotlieb
Peter Grayer
Davis Hall
Louis Haslar
Ruth Hunt
Stanley McGeagh
Stephen D. Newman
John Straub
Alan Thompson
Sarah Venable
Gilbert Vernon

Designed by Norman Coates
Directed by Ed Berman

The play opened for a season at the Collegiate Theatre, London, on 30 July 1979.

Translation from 'Dogg' language into English is given in square brackets where this seems necessary.

Empty stage.

BAKER: (*Off-stage*) Brick! [*Here!]

    (*A football is thrown from off-stage left to off-stage right.*
    BAKER *receiving ball*) Cube. [*Thanks]

    (ABEL, *off-stage, throws satchel to stage left.* ABEL *enters. He is*
    a schoolboy wearing grey flannel shorts, blazer, school cap,
    etc., and carrying a satchel. He drops satchel centre stage and
    collects the other which he places with his own. ABEL *exits stage*
    right and returns with microphone and stand which he places
    down stage. The microphone has a switch.)

ABEL: (*Into the microphone*) Breakfast, breakfast . . . sun—dock—
    trog . . . [*Testing, testing . . . one—two—three . . .]

    (*He realizes the microphone is dead. He tries the switch a*
    couple of times and then speaks again into the microphone.)
    Sun—dock—trog—pan—slack . . . [*One—two—three—
    four—five . . .]

    (*The microphone is still dead.* ABEL *calls to someone off-stage.*)
    Haddock priest! [*The mike is dead!]

    (*Pause.* BAKER *enters from the same direction. He is also a*
    schoolboy similarly dressed.)

BAKER: Eh? [*Eh?]

ABEL: Haddock priest.

BAKER: Haddock?

ABEL: Priest.

    (BAKER *goes to the microphone, drops satchel centre on his way.*)

BAKER: Sun—dock—trog—

    (*The mike is dead.* BAKER *swears.*) Bicycles!

    (BAKER *goes back off-stage. Pause. The loud-speakers crackle.*)

ABEL: Slab? [*Okay?]

BAKER: (*Shouting off-stage, indistinctly.*) Slab!

ABEL: (*Speaking into the mike.*) Sun, dock, trog, slack, pan.

(*The mike is live.* ABEL *shouting to* BAKER, *with a thumbs-up sign.*)

Slab! [*Okay!]

(*Behind* ABEL, CHARLIE, *another schoolboy, enters backwards, hopping about, the visible half of a ball-throwing game.* CHARLIE *is wearing a dress, but schoolboy's shorts, shoes and socks, and no wig.*)

CHARLIE: Brick! . . . brick! [*Here! . . . here!]

(*A ball is thrown to him from the wings.* ABEL *dispossesses* CHARLIE *of the ball.*)

ABEL: Cube! [*Thanks!]

VOICE: (*Off-stage*) Brick! [*Here!)

(CHARLIE *tries to get the ball but* ABEL *won't let him have it.*)

CHARLIE: Squire! [*Bastard!]

(ABEL *throws the ball to the unseen person in the wings—not where* BAKER *is.*)

Daisy squire! [*Mean bastard!]

ABEL: Afternoons! [*Get stuffed!]

CHARLIE: (*Very aggrieved.*) Vanilla squire! [*Rotten bastard!]

ABEL: (*Giving a V-sign to* CHARLIE.) Afternoons!

(ABEL *hopping about, calls for the ball from the wings.*)
Brick! [*Here!]

(*The ball is thrown to* ABEL *over* CHARLIE's *head.* DOGG, *the headmaster, in mortar-board and gown, enters from the opposite wing, and as the ball is thrown to* ABEL, DOGG *dispossesses* ABEL.)

DOGG: Cube! [*Thank you!] Pax! [*Lout!]

(DOGG *gives* ABEL *a clip over the ear and starts to march off carrying the ball.*)

ABEL: (*Respectfully to* DOGG.) Cretinous, git? [*What time it is, sir?]

DOGG: (*Turning round.*) Eh?

ABEL: Cretinous pig-faced, git? [*Have you got the time please, sir?]

(DOGG *takes a watch out of his waistcoat pocket and examines it.*)

DOGG: Trog poxy. [*Half-past three.]

ABEL: Cube, git. [*Thank you, sir.]

16

DOGG: Upside artichoke almost Leamington Spa? [*Have you seen the lorry from Leamington Spa?]

ABEL: Artichoke, git? [*Lorry, sir?]

CHARLIE: Leamington Spa, git? [*Leamington Spa, sir?]

DOGG: Upside? [*Have you seen it?]

ABEL: (*Shaking his head.*) Nit, git. [*No, sir.]

CHARLIE: (*Shaking his head.*) Nit, git. [*No, sir.]

DOGG: (*Leaving again.*) Tsk. Tsk. [*Tsk. Tsk.] Useless. [*Good day.]

ABEL/CHARLIE: Useless, git. [*Good day, sir.]

> (DOGG *exits with the ball.* BAKER *enters. He looks at his wrist watch.*)

BAKER: Trog poxy. [*Half-past three.]

> (*There are now three satchels on the ground centre stage.*
> BAKER *goes to one and extracts a packet of sandwiches.* ABEL
> *and* CHARLIE *do the same. The three boys settle down and start
> to examine their sandwiches.*)

ABEL: (*Looking in his sandwiches.*) Pelican crash. [*Cream cheese.]
(*To* BAKER.) Even ran? [*What have you got?]

BAKER: (*Looking in his sandwich.*) Hollyhocks. [*Ham.]

ABEL: (*To* CHARLIE.) Even ran? [*What have you got?]

CHARLIE: (*Looking in his sandwich.*) Mouseholes. [*Egg.]

ABEL: (*To* CHARLIE.) Undertake sun pelican crash frankly sun mousehole? [*Swop you one cream cheese for one egg?]

CHARLIE: (*With an amiable shrug.*) Slab. [*Okay.]

> (ABEL *and* CHARLIE *exchange half a sandwich each.*)

BAKER: (*To Abel.*) Undertake sun hollyhocks frankly sun pelican crash?

ABEL: Hollyhocks? Nit!

BAKER: Squire!

ABEL: Afternoons!

> (BAKER *fans himself with his cap and makes a comment about
> the heat.*)

BAKER: Afternoons! Phew—cycle racks hardly butter fag ends. [*Comment about heat.]

CHARLIE: (*Agreeing with him.*) Fag ends likely butter consequential.

ABEL: Very true. [*Needs salt.]

CHARLIE: Eh?

ABEL: (*Putting out his hand.*) Very true.

(CHARLIE *takes a salt cellar out of his satchel.* CHARLIE *passes* ABEL *the salt.*)

Cube. [*Thank you.]

(*He sprinkles salt on his sandwich and then offers salt to* BAKER.) Very true? [*Need salt?]

BAKER: (*Taking it.*) Cube. [*Thank you.]

(BAKER *uses the salt and puts it down next to him.* CHARLIE *puts his hand out towards* BAKER.)

CHARLIE: Brick. [*Here.]

(BAKER *passes* CHARLIE *his salt-cellar. They eat their sandwiches. The explanation for the next passage of dialogue is that* ABEL *and* BAKER, *who are due shortly to participate in a school play performed in its original language—English—start rehearsing some of their lines.*)

ABEL: (*Suddenly*) Who's there?

BAKER: Nay, answer me.

ABEL: Long live the King. Get thee to bed.

BAKER: For this relief, much thanks.

(ABEL *stands up.*)

ABEL: What, has this thing appeared again tonight?

(BAKER *stands up by him.*)

BAKER: Peace, break thee off: look where it comes again.

ABEL: Looks it not like the King?

(*They are not acting these lines at all, merely uttering them, tonelessly.*)

BAKER: By heaven, I charge thee, speak!

ABEL: 'Tis here. (*Pointing stage left.*)

BAKER: 'Tis there. (*Pointing stage right, their arms crossing awkwardly.*)

ABEL: 'Tis gone.

BAKER: But look—the russet mantle . . .

(*He has gone wrong. Pause.*)

ABEL: (*Trying to help him.*) Clad—walks . . .

(ABEL *and* BAKER *don't always structure their sentences correctly.*)

BAKER: (*Shakes his head and swears softly to himself.*)

18

Bicycles!

(BAKER *produces from his pocket his script. He looks through it and finds where he has gone wrong.*)

      The *morn*!—the morn in russet mantle clad—walks
      o'er the dew of yon high eastern hill.

ABEL: Let us impart what we have seen tonight unto (*indicating* HAMLET *is just above waist height with his hand.*) young Hamlet . . . Slab? [*Okay?] Block. [*Next.]

(BAKER *shakes his head and sits down.*)

BAKER: (*Shakes head.*) Nit! [*No!]

(CHARLIE, *for no reason, is singing to the tune of 'My Way'. He doesn't know all the words in the third line.* BAKER *joins in on the fourth line in close harmony.*)

CHARLIE: (*Sings*) Engage congratulate moreover state abysmal
      fairground.
      Begat perambulate this aerodrome chocolate eclair
      found.
      Maureen again dedum-de-da- ultimately cried egg.
      Dinosaurs rely indoors if satisfied egg . . .

(ABEL *blows a raspberry by way of judgement. As the song dies away a lorry is heard arriving. The three boys get up and put away their sandwich papers etc. and look expectantly in the direction of the lorry.*)

BAKER: Artichoke. [*Lorry.]

(BAKER *goes forward, looking out into the wings, and starts directing the lorry—which is apparently backing towards him—with expressive gestures.*)

Cauliflower . . . cauliflower . . . hardly . . . onyx hardly . . . [*Left . . . left . . . right . . . right hand down . . .] Tissue . . . tissue . . . slab! [*Straight . . . straight . . . okay!]

(*The lorry-driver* EASY *is heard slamming the cab door and he enters. He is dressed in a white boiler-suit and cloth cap and is carrying a rolled-up red carpet and a box of small flags on sticks. He puts them down.*)

EASY: Buxton's—blocks an' that.

ABEL: Eh?

EASY: Buxton's Deliveries of Leamington Spa. I've got a load of blocks and that. I'll need a bit of a hand.

(Pause. The boys look at him blankly, baffled.)

ABEL: Eh?

EASY: I'll need a bit of a hand, being as I'm on my own, seeing as my mate got struck down in a thunderstorm on the A412 near Rickmansworth—a bizarre accident . . . a bolt from the blue, zig-zagged right on to the perforated snout of his Micky Mouse gas mask. He was delivering five of them at the bacteriological research children's party—entering into the spirit of it—when, shazam!—it was an electrifying moment, left his nose looking more like Donald Duck and his ears like they popped out of a toaster. He sounded like a cuckoo clock striking twelve.

(EASY relates story with considerable gusto, but to his disappointment it falls flat being, of course, not understood.)
Right you are then, lads. Where do you want them?
(Another long pause. BAKER takes a step forward towards EASY, pleased with himself for having a good idea.)

BAKER: By heaven I charge thee speak!
(Pause.)

EASY: Who are you then?

BAKER: *(Encouragingly.)* William Shakespeare.

EASY: *(To ABEL.)* Cretin is he?

BAKER: *(Looking at his wrist watch.)* Trog-taxi.

EASY: I thought so. *(Looking at CHARLIE.)* Are you all a bit peculiar, then? Where's the guvnor?
(DOGG enters briskly.)

DOGG: Useless! [*Afternoon!]

BOYS: Useless, git! [*Afternoon, sir!]

EASY: Afternoon, squire. [This means in Dogg, *Get stuffed, you bastard.]
(DOGG grabs EASY by the lapels in a threatening manner.)

DOGG: Marzipan clocks! [*Watch it!]
(DOGG produces a piece of paper which is a plan of the construction which is to be made on the stage. This is quite a large piece of paper and the steps and wall which are to be built are discernible on it. DOGG examines the paper briefly and then starts positioning the boys.)
Abel . . .

ABEL: Slab, git. [*Yes, sir.]

DOGG: (*Pointing towards the lorry.*) Pontoon crumble.

ABEL: Slab, git.

(ABEL *goes out towards the lorry.*)

DOGG: Baker . . .

(BAKER *pays attention.*)

Brick. [*Here.]

(*He positions* BAKER *next to the wing near the lorry.*)

BAKER: Slab, git.

DOGG: Cube. [*Thank you.] (*To* CHARLIE.) Charlie.

CHARLIE: Slab, git.

DOGG: Brick.

(*He positions* CHARLIE *in line with* BAKER *and the lorry.* EASY *stands next* CHARLIE *in the place where the steps are to be built. To* BAKER *and* CHARLIE.) Plank? [*Ready?]

BAKER/CHARLIE: Plank, git. [*Ready, sir.]

DOGG: (*Calling out to* ABEL.) Plank?

ABEL: (*Off-stage.*) Plank, git.

(DOGG *gives the piece of paper to* EASY *who studies it warily.* EASY *puts the paper in his pocket.*)

DOGG: (*Calling out to* ABEL *loudly—shouts.*) Plank!

(*To* EASY's *surprise and relief a plank is thrown to* BAKER *who catches it, passes it to* CHARLIE, *who passes it to* EASY, *who places it on the stage.* DOGG *smiles, looks encouragingly at* EASY.)

EASY: (*Uncertainly, calls.*) Plank!

To his surprise and relief a second plank is thrown in and passed to him the same way. He places it.)

Plank!

(*A third plank is thrown in and positioned as before.* DOGG *leaves, satisfied. Note:* EASY *is going to build a platform, using 'planks', 'slabs', 'blocks' and 'cubes' so that the platform is stepped, with the steps upstage.*

Confidently, calls.) Plank!

(*A block is thrown instead of a plank. When it reaches* EASY, *he passes it back to* CHARLIE *who passes it back to* BAKER, *who turns and places it on the floor upstage. While* BAKER *is upstage* EASY *has repeated his call.*)

Plank!!

(*A second block is thrown straight into* CHARLIE's *arms.*
CHARLIE *passes it to* EASY *who passes it back to* CHARLIE *who
takes it upstage to join the first block on the floor.* EASY *shouts.*)

Plank!!!

(*A plank is thrown straight to him and he places it gratefully
on the floor next to the other three.* EASY *takes another look at
the plans and replaces them into his pocket. He shouts.*)

Slab!

(BAKER *and* CHARLIE *have resumed their positions. A slab is
thrown in, caught by* BAKER, *passed to* CHARLIE, *passed to* EASY,
who places it on top of the planks. EASY *shouts.*)

Slab!

(*A second slab is thrown in and passed to* EASY *who places it. A
third slab likewise reaches* EASY. *He needs four for his
construction. He shouts.*)

Slab!

(*A block is thrown to* BAKER, *passed to* CHARLIE, *passed to*
EASY, *who impatiently passes it back to* CHARLIE *who passes it
back to* BAKER *who takes it upstage.* EASY *shouts.*)

Slab!

(*Another block is thrown, straight to* CHARLIE *who passes it to*
EASY *who passes it back to* CHARLIE *who walks upstage with it
and places it on the floor.*)

Slab!

ABEL: (*Enters smiling.*) Slab?

EASY: Nit!

ABEL: Nit?

EASY: Git! Slab.

(ABEL *leaves and a moment later another block comes flying
across to* EASY *who catches it, throws it furiously at* BAKER *and*
CHARLIE, *who catch it and put it down.* EASY *walks off into the
wings.*

From his satchel CHARLIE *produces a small transistor radio
which he turns on. He is lucky enough to catch his favourite
song, half-way through the first verse, which we have already
heard.* CHARLIE *sings.*)

EASY: (*Off-stage.*) Useless.

22

ABEL: (*Politely, off-stage.*) Useless, git.

(*There is the sound of a slap and a sharp cry from* ABEL. EASY *re-enters carrying a slab.* DOGG *now re-enters with a tray of button-holes. He puts this down and picks up the box of flags.*)

DOGG: (*Calling off-stage to* ABEL.) Abel!

ABEL: Slab, git.

DOGG: Brick.

(ABEL *enters, holding his ear and glancing aggrievedly at* EASY. DOGG *starts handing out the flags, starting with* ABEL, *who on receiving his flag goes back off-stage.* DOGG *hands flags to* BAKER, CHARLIE *and some of the audience, counting the flags as he gives them out.*)

Sun, dock, trog, slack, pan, sock, slight, bright, none, tun, what, dunce . . .

(EASY, *who has placed the slab and is watching* DOGG, *takes a step towards him.*)

EASY: What?

(DOGG *takes this as a correction.*)

DOGG: Dunce.

EASY: What??

DOGG: Dunce!

EASY: What??

(DOGG *irritably does a re-count, aloud, and finds that he was right . . .*)

DOGG: Sun, dock, trog, slack, pan, sock, slight, bright, none, tun, what, *dunce*!

EASY: Oh!

DOGG: (*Witheringly.*) Pax!

(DOGG *then turns his attention to the button-holes.* EASY *expects to be given one.*)

(*To* EASY.) Nit!

(*He gives a button-hole to* CHARLIE.)

CHARLIE: Cube, git.

DOGG: Block. [*Next.]

(BAKER *comes forward and receives his button-hole.*)

BAKER: Cube, git.

DOGG: (*Calls out to* ABEL.) Block! Abel!

(ABEL *comes on and receives his button-hole.* ABEL *is holding his*

23

ear in an aggrieved manner, looking at EASY.)

ABEL: Cube, git.

(ABEL *retires back to the lorry.* DOGG *looks expectantly at* EASY.)

DOGG: Slab? [*Okay?]

EASY: Block.

DOGG: Slab.

EASY: Block.

DOGG: Slab.

(*He obviously expects* EASY *to carry on with the work.* EASY *re-examines the plan, replaces it in his pocket and nervously calls out to* ABEL.)

EASY: Block!

(*To his surprise and relief a block is thrown in. By this time* CHARLIE, *who had guiltily turned off the radio as soon as* DOGG *entered, has gone back to his receiving position, as has* BAKER. *The block is passed down the line to* EASY *who places it on top of the slabs. He calls out.*)

Block!

(*Another block follows the same route.* DOGG *leaves satisfied.* EASY *calls out.*)

Block!

(*A slab is heaved on.* BAKER *catches it and passes it to* CHARLIE *who, however, anticipates* EASY's *reaction and takes it back upstage to join the blocks on the floor.* EASY *shouts out.*)

Block!

(*Another slab is heaved on and* BAKER *no less astutely takes it upstage.* EASY *marches off towards* ABEL.)

CHARLIE: Cretin is he?

BAKER: Cretin is he?—Trog—taxi—marmalade. [*Marmalade denotes pleasure and approval.]

EASY: (*Off-stage.*) Great Oaf!

ABEL: Git?

(*This is followed by another cry of pain from* ABEL. CHARLIE *has turned his radio on again. The radio emits the familiar pips of the time signal.* BAKER *checks his watch.*)

RADIO: Check mumble hardly out. [*Here are the football results.]

(CHARLIE *takes a pools coupon out of his satchel and starts*

24

checking it off. The rhythm of the language coming out of the
radio is the familiar one, appropriate to home wins, away wins,
and draws.
The following is a translation of the numbers;

Nil = quite	*3 = trog*
1 = sun	*4 = slack*
2 = dock	*5 = pan*

In addition, 'Clock' and 'Foglamp' correspond to 'City' and
'United'. Thus the result, 'Haddock Clock quite, Haddock
Foglamp trog' would be delivered with the inflections appropriate
to, say, 'Manchester City nil, Manchester United three'—an
away win. The radio starts by saying, 'Oblong Sun' with the
inflection of 'Division One'.)

RADIO: Oblong Sun, Dogtrot quite, Flange dock; Cabrank dock,
Blanket Clock quite; Tube Clock dock, Handbag dock;
Haddock Clock quite, Haddock Foglamp trog; Wonder
quite, Picknicking pan . . .

(CHARLIE whistles at that—a five-nil away win. Meanwhile
EASY re-enters carrying a tall load of blocks, followed by ABEL,
limping, carrying a similar load. EASY puts his blocks down. He
notices the radio and CHARLIE checking his pools. EASY produces
a pools coupon and a pencil before he realizes that he can't
make head or tail of the radio.)

EASY: *(Bemused.)* Do you mind if I ask you something. What
wavelength are you on?

(Meanwhile BAKER has started to make a neat wall out of the
blocks and slabs which have so far been assembled. It is
apparent now that some of the blocks have got apparently
random letters printed on them. EASY, having put away his
pools coupon, adds blocks to the steps. ABEL has dumped his
load of blocks near BAKER and now limps off stage back to the
lorry. DOGG enters.)

DOGG: *(To EASY.)* Moronic creep. [*Maroon carpet.]

(EASY grabs DOGG by the lapel.)

EASY: Watch it!

(DOGG, surprised, disengages himself.)

DOGG: *(To EASY.)* Afternoons—moronic creep?

BAKER: *(To DOGG.)* Brick, git. [*Here, sir.]

DOGG: Ah. Cube.

(BAKER *points at the carpet.* DOGG *unrolls the red carpet to make a path from the microphone to the wings.* CHARLIE *has turned off the radio on* DOGG's *entrance and now* BAKER *rejoins him in building the wall.* EASY *has completed that stage of the steps, and the wall is complete.* BAKER *and* CHARLIE *are nowhere to be seen because they built the wall from the back and it now conceals them. This leaves* EASY *apparently alone in front of the wall. He hasn't yet noticed the letters, which read;*

MATHS

OLD

EGG

EASY *takes the plan out of his pocket and studies it again.* DOGG *notices the wall. He looks at* EASY. EASY *looks at the wall.* EASY *looks at* DOGG. EASY *smiles.* DOGG *slaps* EASY *lightly on the cheek.* EASY *opens his mouth to protest.* DOGG *cuffs him heavily on the other cheek and knocks* EASY *through the wall which disintegrates.* DOGG *takes the piece of paper out of* EASY's *pocket and looks at it carefully.* EASY *picks himself up.* CHARLIE *and* BAKER *go back into their receiving positions.* DOGG *gives the paper back to* EASY.)

EASY: Here, what's your game?

DOGG: Cube. [*Thank you.]

EASY: Eh?

DOGG: Cube.

(*Then he calls out to* ABEL.)

Cube! Abel!

(*A cube is thrown in to* BAKER, *passed to* CHARLIE, *passed to* EASY *who puts it in place.* DOGG *to* CHARLIE *and* BAKER.) Slab?

EASY: Cube.

DOGG: Slab.

CHARLIE/BAKER: Cube, git!

EASY: (*With venom.*) Git!

(DOGG *is pleased and smiles.* EASY *is completely at a loss.* DOGG *leaves satisfied.*)

Cube!

(*Another cube follows the same route.*)

Cube!

26

(*A slab sails on and* BAKER *and* CHARLIE *catch it together. They immediately take it upstage and place it down to form the base of a rebuilt wall. They start rebuilding the wall. Meanwhile* EASY *walks off towards* ABEL *and as soon as he is off-stage there is the sound of a thump and a cry from* ABEL. ABEL *walks on, limping, holding his ear and rubbing his backside.*)

EASY: (*Off-stage.*) Cube!

(*A cube sails on over* ABEL'*s head, and* ABEL, *who is caught by surprise, catches it and places it on the steps. This keeps happening again and again while* BAKER *and* CHARLIE *rebuild the wall.* ABEL, *however, makes a tower out of the cubes instead of laying them to make a new level. After seven cubes, in toto,* EASY *enters and sees the tottering tower of cubes and just saves them from collapsing.* BAKER *and* CHARLIE *meanwhile have removed themselves from view by rebuilding the wall which now says;*

MEG

SHOT

GLAD

DOGG *enters, carrying a small table with silver trophies covered with a velvet cloth. He walks to the microphone and tests it.*)

DOGG: Sun, dock, trogg . . .

(*The microphone is dead.* DOGG *to* BAKER.)

Haddock priest.

BAKER: Haddock, git?

DOGG: Priest.

(BAKER *goes to the microphone and turns the switch on.*)

Sun, dock, trog . . . Gymshoes. [*Excellent.]

(*The microphone is live. Meanwhile* EASY *has placed all the cubes correctly so that they make a top layer to the steps. He is one cube short, however.* ABEL *goes back to the lorry.*)

EASY: Cube short.

DOGG: (*To* EASY.) Brick?

EASY: Cube!

DOGG: Brick.

EASY: Cube!

(*A cube sails in from the lorry and* EASY *catches it and then the steps are complete.* DOGG *turns to go, sees the new wall with its message and looks at* EASY. EASY *looks at the wall. He looks at* DOGG.)

Pax!

(DOGG *knocks him through the wall which disintegrates.* DOGG *leaves.* CHARLIE *and* BAKER *start re-assembling the components of the wall.* EASY *shouts after* DOGG.)

Yob! [*Flowers.]

(CHARLIE, BAKER *and* EASY *are roughly in line by the carpet.* DOGG *reappears immediately with a bouquet which is wrapped in cellophane and tied with a red ribbon. It is important that it is distinctive because it appears in the second half of the play. He hands this to* CHARLIE. *March music is heard.* CHARLIE *gives the bouquet to* BAKER *who gives it to* EASY *who thrusts it into* DOGG's *hands as he exits.* DOGG *re-enters furiously and gives flowers back to* EASY *who gives them to* ABEL *as he enters.* ABEL *gives them to* CHARLIE *who loses them while rebuilding the wall.* EASY *exits and returns with lid for platform.* CHARLIE *and* BAKER, *now joined by* ABEL, *rebuild the wall, then take their little flags out of their pockets and start waving them.* EASY *joins in unhappily.*

A LADY *enters followed by a smirking* DOGG. *The music plays, the flags wave. The* LADY *gets to the microphone. The music stops and she is ready to give her speech which is written on a neat postcard held in her gloved hand.*)

LADY: (*Nicely.*) Scabs, slobs, yobs, yids, spicks, wops . . .

(*As one might say Your Grace, ladies and gentlemen, boys and girls . . .*)

Sad fact, brats pule puke crap-pot stink, spit; grow up dunces crooks; rank socks dank snotrags, conkers, ticks; crib books, cock snooks, block bogs, jack off, catch pox pick spots, scabs, padlocks, seek kicks, kinks, slack; nick swag, swig coke, bank kickbacks; . . . frankly can't stick kids. Mens sana in corpore sano.

(*Applause.* LADY *comes down from the platform helped by* DOGG. *They stand by the table.* DOGG *lifts the cloth to reveal the school trophies.*)

DOGG: (*Presenting school prizes reads.*) Pansticks jammy, sun-up—Fox Major.

28

(FOX *enters from auditorium left, climbs steps to stage and collects his prize. He shakes hands with a beaming* LADY.)

FOX: Cube, get. [*Thank you, madam.]

(FOX *exits into auditorium right.*)

DOGG: As Grimsby primate what, sun-up—Fox Major.

(FOX, *still near the front of the auditorium, turns and awkwardly squeezes in between two rows of seats. As he steps over the audience's legs he apologetically exclaims 'Cutlery' [*Excuse me], reaches stage and receives prize as before.*)

Cuff-laces empty cross . . . Crazy jogs . . . Poodle-fire . . . Melon legs arc lamps . . . pelvic wiggle stamp . . . grinning . . . grape-soot pergolas . . . fairly pricks double . . . elegant frantically . . . plugs . . . Fox Major.

(DOGG *has been placing all these trophies on top of the velvet which covered them earlier, and which he has placed on the platform* EASY *built.* FOX *whoops when he hears his name and rushes onto the stage as before, but picks up the table, which is now quite bare, and exits trimphantly stage left.*

Throughout this presentation ABLE, BAKER *and* CHARLIE *have been waving their flags each time* FOX *arrives on stage, but their faces reveal their dissatisfaction and boredom.*)

Practically . . . Helmet bedsocks Denmark. [*And now . . . Helmet Prince of Denmark.]

MRS DOGG (*Correcting him.*) Hamlet . . .

DOGG: Hamlet bedsocks Denmark, yeti William Shakespeare. (*To* MRS DOGG.) Yob?

MRS DOGG: Yob . . . yob . . . yob? [*Flowers?]

(*She looks to schoolboys, who know nothing of their whereabouts.* MRS DOGG *turns away and gives* LADY *her button-hole, with a little curtsey. To* LADY.)

Hernia, suppurating kidneys, reeks cat-boils frankly gangrenous armpit dripping maggots . . .

LADY: (*With energy and charm.*) Sod the pudding club!

(*Music.* DOGG, MRS DOGG *and* LADY *begin to exit past the wall. The* LADY *notices the message on the wall which says:*

GOD
SLAG
THEM

She is taken aback but bravely continues out. DOGG *looks daggers at* EASY. *As soon as the* LADY *and* MRS DOGG *have left the stage* DOGG *does an about-turn and marches back to* EASY. EASY *looks at* DOGG. DOGG *looks at the wall.* EASY *dutifully hurls himself through the wall which disintegrates.* DOGG *leaves.* EASY *picks himself up. He shouts furiously after* DOGG.)

EASY: Stinkbag! Poxy crank!

(ABEL, BAKER *and* CHARLIE *are also resentful about* DOGG *and all their succeeding lines, as are* EASY's, *are insults referring to* DOGG, *though not necessarily called out after him.*)

BAKER: Pax! Quinces carparks!

EASY: Canting poncey creep!

CHARLIE: Daisy squire!

EASY: Sadist! Fascist!

ABEL: Fishes! Afternoons!

EASY: Officious bastard! Lunatic!

ABEL: Avacados castle sofa Dogg!

EASY: Have his guts for garters, see if I don't!

ABEL: (*Talking to* EASY *about* DOGG.) Avocados castle cigar smoke.

EASY: (*To* ABLE.) Right!—See if I don't! Kick his backside!

BAKER: (*To* EASY.) Quinces ice-packs!

EASY: (*To* BAKER.) Right!

CHARLIE: Daisy squire!

BAKER: Slab git, nit git—

EASY: Three bags full git! Crazy little squirt!

CHARLIE: Daisy vanilla!

EASY: Squire! Quince bog! Have his pax for carpox—so help me Dogg, see avocado!——Slab.

BAKER: Moronic creep.

EASY: Slab. Cretinous pig-face?

BAKER: Cretinous pig-face? Slack-dunce. [*4: 10.]

EASY: What?

BAKER: Dunce.

EASY: Cube.

(*During the above* ABEL, BAKER *and* CHARLIE *have been rebuilding the wall, and* EASY *has been rolling up the red carpet. Now* EASY *starts collecting all the flags back starting with the three flags given to* ABEL, BAKER *and* CHARLIE *which*

30

they threw to the floor in disgust. He collects flags from the audience and counts them as he collects them, and thanks each one, 'Cube', as he does so.)

Sun, dock, trog, slack, pan, sock, slight, bright, none, fun, what, dunce!

(ABEL, BAKER *and* CHARLIE *have just finished building the wall and have built themselves out of view.* EASY *moves to exit, when we hear . . .)*

BAKER: (*From behind screen and pointing at microphone.*) Haddock.
(EASY *returns and takes off microphone. Before he exits . . .)*

EASY: Hamlet bedsocks Denmark. Yeti William Shakespeare.
(*The wall says:*

DOGGS
HAM
LET

The lighting changes and there is a trumpet fanfare and DOGG *enters now dressed to take his part in the* 15-Minute Hamlet. *He goes to the platform, from which he speaks the prologue of the* Hamlet, *and then exits. This leaves the wall and the steps to be used as the walls and ramparts of Elsinore. At the back of the stage left and right are two folding screens. The stage left screen has a bolt through the top which allows a cut-out sun, moon and crown to be swung into vision from behind the screen. From the on-stage side pivots a two-dimensional cut-out grave for* OPHELIA.)

PROLOGUE

Enter SHAKESPEARE, *bows.*

SHAKESPEARE: For this relief, much thanks.
Though I am native here, and to the manner born,
It is a custom more honoured in the breach
Than in the observance
Well.
Something is rotten in the state of Denmark.
To be, or not to be, that is the question.
There are more things in heaven and earth
Than are dreamt of in your philosophy—

There's a divinity that shapes our ends,
Rough hew them how we will
Though this be madness, yet there is method in it.
I must be cruel only to be kind;
Hold, as t'were, the mirror up to nature.
A countenance more in sorrow than in anger.
(LADY *in audience shouts 'Marmalade'.*)
The lady doth protest too much.
Cat will mew, and Dogg will have his day!
(*Bows and exits. End of prologue.*)

A castle battlement. Thunder and wind. Enter two GUARDS: BERNARDO/
MARCELLUS *and* FRANCISCO/HORATIO. *The* GUARDS *are played by* ABEL
and BAKER *respectively. They are costumed for a typical Shakespeare
play except that they have short trousers.* GUARDS *on the platform.*

BERNARDO: Who's there?
FRANCISCO: Nay, answer me.
BERNARDO: Long live the King. Get thee to bed.
FRANCISCO: For this relief, much thanks.
BERNARDO: What, has this thing appeared again tonight?
FRANCISCO: Peace, break thee off: look where it comes again!
BERNARDO: Looks it not like the King?
FRANCISCO: By heaven, I charge thee, speak!
BERNARDO: (*Points and looks left.*) 'Tis here.
FRANCISCO: (*Points and looks right.*) 'Tis there.
BERNARDO: (*Looks right.*) 'Tis gone.
FRANCISCO: But look, the morn in russet mantle clad
       Walks o'er the dew of yon high eastern hill.
       (*On 'But look' a cut-out sun shoots up over the stage
       left screen, and descends here.*)
BERNARDO: Let us impart what we have seen tonight
       Unto young Hamlet.
       (*Exeunt. End scene.*)

*A room of state within the castle. A cut-out crown hinges over stage
left screen.*

32

Flourish of trumpets. Enter CLAUDIUS *and* GERTRUDE, *who is played by* MRS DOGG.

CLAUDIUS: Though yet of Hamlet our dear brother's death
    The memory be green
    (*Enter* HAMLET *who is played by* FOX MAJOR.)
    Our sometime sister, now our Queen
    Have we taken to wife.
    But now, my cousin Hamlet, and my son—
HAMLET: A little more than kin, and less than kind.
    (*Exit* CLAUDIUS *and* GERTRUDE.)
    O that this too too solid flesh would melt!
    That it should come to this—but two months dead!
    So loving to my mother: Frailty, thy name is
     woman!
    Married with mine uncle, my father's brother.
    The funeral baked meats did coldly furnish forth
    The marriage tables.
    (*The crown hinges down.* HORATIO *rushes on.*)
HORATIO: My lord, I think I saw him yesternight—
    The King, your father—upon the platform where
     we watched.
HAMLET: 'Tis very strange.
HORATIO: Armed, my lord—
    A countenance more in sorrow than in anger.
HAMLET: My father's spirit in arms? All is not well.
    Would the night were come!
    (*The moon hinges up. Exeunt to parapet. End scene.*)

The castle battlements at night. Noise of carouse, cannon, fireworks.
HORATIO *and* HAMLET *appear on platform built by* EASY.

HAMLET: The King doth wake tonight and takes his rouse,
    Though I am native here and to the manner born,
    It is a custom more honoured in the breach
    Than in the observance.
    (*Wind noise.*)
HORATIO: Look, my lord, it comes. (*Points*)
    (*Enter* GHOST *above the wall built of blocks.*)

B

HAMLET: Angels and ministers of grace defend us!
Something is rotten in the state of Denmark!
Alas, poor ghost.
GHOST: I am thy father's spirit.
Revenge his foul and most unnnatural murder.
HAMLET: Murder?
GHOST: The serpent that did sting thy father's life
Now wears his crown.
HAMLET: O my prophetic soul? Mine uncle?
(*Exit* GHOST. *To* HORATIO.)
There are more things in heaven and earth
Than are dreamt of in your philosophy.
(*Exit* HORATIO.)
Hereafter I shall think meet
To put an antic disposition on.
The time is out of joint. O cursed spite
That ever I was born to set it right!
(*Exit* HAMLET. *Moon hinges down. End scene.*)

A room within. Crown hinges up. Flourish of trumpets leading into flute and harpsichord music. Enter POLONIUS; OPHELIA *rushes on.* OPHELIA *is, of course, played by* CHARLIE.

POLONIUS: How now Ophelia, what's the matter?
OPHELIA: My lord, as I was sewing in my chamber,
Lord Hamlet with his doublet all unbraced;
No hat upon his head, pale as his shirt,
His knees knocking each other, and with a look so
piteous
He comes before me.
POLONIUS: Mad for thy love?
I have found the very cause of Hamlet's lunacy.
(*Enter* HAMLET, *exit* OPHELIA.)
Look where sadly the poor wretch comes reading
What do you read, my lord?
HAMLET: Words, words, words.
POLONIUS: Though this be madness, yet there is method in it.
HAMLET: I am but mad north northwest: when the wind is

southerly I know a hawk from a
handsaw.
(*Slams book shut and against* POLONIUS's *chest.*)
POLONIUS: The actors are come hither, my lord. (*Exits*)
HAMLET: We'll hear a play tomorrow.
I have heard that guilty creatures sitting at a play
Have by the very cunning of the scene
Been struck so to the soul that presently
They have proclaimed their malefactions.
I'll have these players play something
Like the murder of my father before mine uncle.
If he but blench, I know my course.
The play's the thing
Wherein I'll catch the conscience of the King.
(*Pause*)
To be, or not to be (*Puts dagger, pulled from his
sleeve, to heart.*
Enter CLAUDIUS *and* OPHELIA.)
that is the question.
OPHELIA: My lord—
HAMLET: Get thee to a nunnery!
(*Exit* OPHELIA *and* HAMLET.)
CLAUDIUS: Love? His affections do not that way tend
There's something in his soul
O'er which his melancholy sits on brood.
He shall with speed to England.
(*Exit* CLAUDIUS. *End scene.*)

A hall within the castle. Flourish of trumpets. Enter HAMLET *and*
OPHELIA, MARCELLUS *and* HORATIO *joking,* CLAUDIUS *and* GERTRUDE.
Puppet players appear above stage left screen.
HAMLET: (*To puppet players.*) Speak the speech, I pray you, as I
pronounced it to you; trippingly on the tongue.
Hold, as t'were, the mirror up to nature
(ALL *sit to watch puppet play. Masque music*)
(*To* GERTRUDE.) Madam, how like you the play?
GERTRUDE: The lady doth protest too much, methinks.

HAMLET: He poisons him in the garden of his estate. You shall see anon how the murderer gets the love of Gonzago's wife.
(CLAUDIUS *rises.*)
The King rises!
(*Music stops, hubbub noise starts.*)
What, frighted with false fire?
(*Exit,* CLAUDIUS.)
ALL: Give o'er the play.
(*Puppets disappear, crown disappears.*)
HAMLET: Lights! Lights! Lights! I'll take the ghost's word for a thousand pounds!
(*Exeunt* ALL *except* POLONIUS.)
POLONIUS: (*Standing at side.*) He's going to his mother's closet. Behind the arras I'll convey myself to hear the process.
(*End scene.*)

The Queen's apartment. POLONIUS *stands by stage right screen and hinges a curtain out from behind it. Lute music. Enter* HAMLET *and* GERTRUDE.

HAMLET: Now Mother, what's the matter?
GERTRUDE: Hamlet, thou hast thy father much offended.
HAMLET: Mother, you have my father much offended.
(*Holds her.*)
GERTRUDE: What wilt thou do? Thou wilt not murder me? Help! Help! Ho!
POLONIUS: (*Behind the arras.*) Help!
HAMLET: How now? A rat? (*Stabs* POLONIUS.) Dead for a ducat, dead!
GERTRUDE: O me, what hast thou done?
HAMLET: Nay, I know not.
GERTRUDE: Alas, he's mad.
HAMLET: I must be cruel only to be kind. Good night, Mother.
(*Exit* HAMLET *dragging* POLONIUS. *Exit* GERTRUDE, *sobbing. Arras hinges back. End scene.*)

36

Another room in the castle. Flourish of trumpets. Crown hinges up.
Enter CLAUDIUS *and* HAMLET.

CLAUDIUS: Now, Hamlet, where's Polonius?

HAMLET: At supper. (*Hiding his sword clumsily.*)

CLAUDIUS: Hamlet, this deed must send thee hence.
　　　　　Therefore prepare thyself,
　　　　　Everything is bent for England.
　　　　　(*Exit* HAMLET.)
　　　　　And England, if my love thou holds't at aught,
　　　　　Thou may'st not coldly set our sov'reign process,
　　　　　The present death of Hamlet. Do it, England!
　　　　　(*Exit* CLAUDIUS. *Crown hingest down. End scene.*)

At sea.
Sea music. A sail appears above stage left screen. Enter HAMLET *on*
platform, swaying as if on ship's bridge. He wipes his eyes, and becomes
seasick. End sea music. Exit HAMLET, *holding his hand to his mouth.*

Yet another room in the castle. Flourish of trumpets. Enter CLAUDIUS
and LAERTES.

LAERTES: Where is my father?

CLAUDIUS: Dead.
　　　　　(*Enter* OPHELIA *in mad trance, singing and carrying a bouquet*
　　　　　of flowers wrapped in cellophane and with a red ribbon. Lute
　　　　　music.)

OPHELIA: They bore him barefaced on the bier,
　　　　　(*After her first line she gives a flower to* LAERTES.)
　　　　　Hey nonny nonny, hey nonny.
　　　　　(*After her second, she slams the bouquet in* CLAUDIUS'S
　　　　　stomach. It is, of course, the missing bouquet from the
　　　　　speech-day ceremony.)

OPHELIA: And on his grave rained many a tear . . .
　　　　　(*Half-way through her third line she disappears behind*
　　　　　the screen stage left and pauses. CLAUDIUS *and* LAERTES
　　　　　peer round the side she disappeared and she runs round
　　　　　the other behind them.)

37

LAERTES: O heat dry up my brains—O kind Sister,
(OPHELIA *falls to ground. She catches a flower thrown from stage right screen.*)
Had'st thou thy wits, and did'st persuade revenge
It could not move thus.

CLAUDIUS: And where the offence is, let the great axe fall.
(*Exit* CLAUDIUS *and* LAERTES. OPHELIA *sits up to reach gravestone which she swings down to conceal her. Bell tolls four times. End scene.*)

A churchyard. Enter GRAVEDIGGER *and* HAMLET.

HAMLET: Ere we were two days at sea, a pirate of very warlike appointment gave us chase. In the grapple I boarded them. On the instant they got clear of our ship; so I alone became their prisoner. They have dealt with me like thieves of mercy.

GRAVEDIGGER: What is he that builds stronger than either the mason, the shipwright or the carpenter?

HAMLET: A gravemaker. The houses he makes will last till Doomsday.
(GRAVEDIGGER *gives skull to* HAMLET.)
Whose was it?

GRAVEDIGGER: This same skull, Sir, was Yorick's skull, the King's jester.

HAMLET: Alas, poor Yorick. (*Returns skull to* GRAVEDIGGER.)
But soft—that is Laertes. (*Withdraws to side.*)
(*Enter* LAERTES.)

LAERTES: What ceremony else?
Lay her in the earth,
May violets spring. I tell thee, churlish priest . . .
(*Enter* CLAUDIUS *and* GERTRUDE.)
A ministering angel shall my sister be
When thou liest howling.

HAMLET: (*Hiding behind the brick platform.*) What, the fair Ophelia?

LAERTES: O treble woe. Hold off the earth awhile,
Till I have caught her once more in my arms.

HAMLET: (*Re-entering acting area.*)
What is he whose grief bears such an emphasis?
This is I, Hamlet the Dane!
LAERTES: The devil take thy soul.
(*They grapple.*)
HAMLET: Away thy hand!
(CLAUDIUS *and* GERTRUDE *pull them apart.*)
CLAUDIUS/GERTRUDE: Hamlet! Hamlet!
HAMLET: I loved Ophelia. What wilt thou do for her?
GERTRUDE: O he is mad. Laertes!
(*Exit* CLAUDIUS, GERTRUDE *and* LAERTES.)
HAMLET: The cat will mew, and dog will have his day!
(*Exeunt. End scene.*)

A hall in the castle. Flourish of trumpets, crown hinges up.
Enter HAMLET.
HAMLET: There's a divinity that shapes our ends, rough hew
them how we will. But thou would'st not think how
ill all's here about my heart. But 'tis no matter. We
defy augury. There is a special providence in the
fall of a sparrow. If it be now, 'tis not to come; if it
be not to come, it will be now; if it be not now, yet
it will come. The readiness is all.
(LAERTES *enters with* OSRIC *bearing swords followed by*
CLAUDIUS *and* GERTRUDE *with goblets.*)
Come on, Sir!
LAERTES: Come, my lord.
(*Fanfare of trumpets. They draw and duel.*)
HAMLET: One.
LAERTES: No.
HAMLET: Judgement?
OSRIC: A hit, a very palpable hit.
CLAUDIUS: Stay, give me a drink.
Hamlet, this pearl is thine, here's to thy health.
(*Drops pearl in goblet.*)
Give him the cup.
GERTRUDE: The Queen carouses to thy fortune, Hamlet.

CLAUDIUS: Gertrude, do not drink!
GERTRUDE: I will, my lord. (*Drinks*)
LAERTES: My lord, I'll hit him now.
Have at you, now!
(*The grapple and fight.*)
CLAUDIUS: Part them, they are incensed.
They bleed on both sides.
(OSRIC *and* CLAUDIUS *part them.*)
LAERTES: I am justly killed by my own treachery. (*Falls*)
GERTRUDE: The drink, the drink! I am poisoned! (*Dies*)
HAMLET: Treachery! Seek it out.
(*Enter* FORTINBRAS.)
LAERTES: It is here, Hamlet. Hamlet thou art slain.
Lo, here I lie, never to rise again.
The King, the King's to blame.
HAMLET: The point envenomed too?
Then venom to thy work. (*Kills* CLAUDIUS.)
(*Crown hinges down.*)
LAERTES: Exchange forgiveness with me, noble Ha . . . m . . .
(*Dies*)
HAMLET: I follow thee.
I cannot live to hear the news from England.
The rest is silence. (*Dies*)
HORATIO: Good night sweet prince,
And flights of angels sing thee to thy rest.
(*Turns to face away from audience.*)
Go, bid the soldiers shoot.
(*Four shots heard from off-stage.* ALL *stand, bow once and exit. End.*)

THE ENCORE

Encore signs appear above each screen. Flourish of trumpets, crown hinges up. Enter CLAUDIUS *and* GERTRUDE.

CLAUDIUS: Our sometime sister, now our Queen,
(*Enter* HAMLET.)
Have we taken to wife.

(Crown hinges down.)

HAMLET: That it should come to this!
(Exit CLAUDIUS and GERTRUDE. Wind noise. Moon hinges up. Enter HORATIO above.)

HORATIO: My lord, I saw him yesternight—
The King, your father.

HAMLET: Angels and ministers of grace defend us!
(Exit, running, through rest of speech.)
Something is rotten in the state of Denmark.
(Enter GHOST above.)

GHOST: I am thy father's spirit.
The serpent that did sting thy father's life
(Enter HAMLET above.)
Now wears his crown.

HAMLET: O my prophetic soul!
Hereafter I shall think meet
To put an antic disposition on.
(Moon hinges down. Exeunt.
Short flourish of trumpets. Enter POLONIUS below, running. Crown hinges up.)

POLONIUS: Look where sadly the poor wretch comes.
(Exit POLONIUS, running. Enter HAMLET.)

HAMLET: I have heard that guilty creatures sitting at a play
Have by the very cunning of the scene been struck.
(Enter CLAUDIUS, GERTRUDE, OPHELIA, MARCELLUS and HORATIO joking. ALL sit to watch imaginary play, puppets appear above screen.)
If he but blench, I know my course.
(Masque music. CLAUDIUS rises.)
The King rises!

ALL: Give o'er the play!
(Exeunt ALL except GERTRUDE and HAMLET. Crown hinges down.)

HAMLET: I'll take the ghost's word for a thousand pounds.
(Enter POLONIUS, goes behind arras. Short flourish of trumpets.)
Mother, you have my father much offended.

GERTRUDE: Help!

POLONIUS: Help, Ho!

HAMLET: (*Stabs* POLONIUS.) Dead for a ducat, dead!
(POLONIUS *falls dead off-stage. Exit* GERTRUDE *and*
HAMLET. *Short flourish of trumpets. Enter* CLAUDIUS
followed by HAMLET.)

CLAUDIUS: Hamlet, this deed must send thee hence
(*Exit* HAMLET.)
Do it, England.
(*Exit* CLAUDIUS. *Enter* OPHELIA, *falls to ground. Rises
and pulls gravestone to cover herself. Bell tolls twice.
Enter* GRAVEDIGGER *and* HAMLET.)

HAMLET: A pirate gave us chase. I alone became their prisoner.
(*Takes skull from* GRAVEDIGGER.)
Alas poor Yorick—but soft (*Returns skull to*
GRAVEDIGGER.)—This is I,
Hamlet the Dane!
(*Exit* GRAVEDIGGER. *Enter* LAERTES.)

LAERTES: The devil take thy soul!
(*They grapple, then break. Enter* OSRIC *between them
with swords. They draw. Crown hinges up. Enter*
CLAUDIUS *and* GERTRUDE *with goblets.*)

HAMLET: Come on, Sir!
(LAERTES *and* HAMLET *fight.*)

OSRIC: A hit, a very palpable hit!

CLAUDIUS: Give him the cup. Gertrude, do not drink!

GERTRUDE: I am poisoned! (*Dies*)

LAERTES: Hamlet, thou art slain! (*Dies*)

HAMLET: Then venom to thy work! (*Kills* CLAUDIUS.
Crown hinges down.)
The rest is silence. (*Dies*)
(*Two shots off-stage. End*)

The actors stand up to take their curtain call. While this is going on
EASY *walks on whistling, lifts lid from steps, removes a cube and walks
off with it. The actors retire.*

EASY: (*To audience.*) Cube . . .
(*He walks out.*)

Cahoot's Macbeth

Characters

The shortened *Macbeth* has not been organized for any specific number of actors. Ideally it would be done without much in the way of doubling, but it may be done with a minimum of three male and two female actors. In the Czech productions, Kohout distributed the roles as follows (I have not used Donalbain, Wounded Captain, Macduff's wife, or a second messenger):

FIRST ACTOR	Macbeth
SECOND ACTOR	Duncan, Banquo, Macduff, 1st Murderer, Messenger
THIRD ACTOR	Ross, Malcolm, 2nd Murderer, 3rd Witch
FIRST ACTRESS	2nd Witch, Servant
SECOND ACTRESS	Lady Macbeth, 1st Witch

The action takes place in the living room of a flat.
Thunder and lightning. Three WITCHES *in minimal light.*

1ST WITCH: When shall we three meet again?
In thunder, lightning, or in rain?
2ND WITCH: When the hurly-burly's done,
When the battle's lost and won.
3RD WITCH: That will be ere the set of sun.
1ST WITCH: Where the place?
2ND WITCH: Upon the heath.
3RD WITCH: There to meet with Macbeth.
ALL: Fair is foul, and foul is fair.
Hover through the fog and filthy air.
(*Four drum beats.*)
3RD WITCH: A drum! a drum!
Macbeth doth come.
(*Enter* MACBETH *and* BANQUO.)
MACBETH: So foul and fair a day I have not seen.
BANQUO: How far is't called to Forres? What are these, so
withered and so wild in their attire, That look
not like the inhabitants o'the earth, And yet are
on't?
MACBETH: Speak if you can! What are you?
(*The* WITCHES *encircle* MACBETH.)
1ST WITCH: All hail, Macbeth! Hail to thee, Thane of
Glamis!
2ND WITCH: All hail, Macbeth! Hail to thee, Thane of
Cawdor!
3RD WITCH: All hail, Macbeth, that shalt be king hereafter!
BANQUO: Speak then to me who neither beg nor fear
Your favours nor your hate.

3RD WITCH: Thou shalt get kings, though thou be none.
So all hail, Macbeth and Banquo!

1ST WITCH: Banquo and Macbeth, all hail!
(*The* WITCHES *vanish.*)

MACBETH: Stay, you imperfect speakers! Tell me more!

BANQUO: Wither are they vanished?
(*Lights up to reveal living room.*)

MACBETH: Into the air;
Would they had stayed!

BANQUO: Were such things here as we do speak about?
Or have we eaten on the insane root
That takes the reason prisoner?

MACBETH: Your children shall be kings.

BANQUO: You shall be king.

MACBETH: And Thane of Cawdor too, went it not so?

BANQUO: To the selfsame tune and words.
(*Enter* ROSS.)
Who's there?

ROSS: The King hath happily received, Macbeth,
The news of thy success. I am sent
To give thee from our royal master thanks;
And for an earnest of a greater honour,
He bade me from him call thee Thane of
Cawdor.

BANQUO: What! Can the devil speak true?

MACBETH: The Thane of Cawdor lives. Why do you dress
me
In borrowed robes?

ROSS: Who was the Thane lives yet;
But treasons capital, confessed, and proved
Have overthrown him.
(ROSS *hands* MACBETH *a chain and seal which were
Cawdor's.*)

MACBETH: (*Aside*) Glamis, and Thane of Cawdor!
The greatest is behind. Two truths are told
As happy prologues to the swelling Act
Of the imperial theme—I thank you, gentlemen.

ROSS: My worthy Cawdor!

(*Exit* ROSS *and* BANQUO.)
MACBETH: (*Aside*) Stars hide your fires,
Let not light see my black and deep desires.
(*Exit* MACBETH.
Drums.
Enter LADY MACBETH *reading a letter.*)
LADY MACBETH: (*Reading aloud to herself.*) 'Whiles I stood rapt in
the wonder of it, came missives from the King,
who all-hailed me, "Thane of Cawdor"; by
which title, before, these weird sisters saluted me,
and referred me to the coming on of time, with
"Hail, king that shalt be." This have I thought
good to deliver thee, my dearest partner of
greatness, that thou mightest not lose the dues of
rejoicing by being ignorant of what greatness is
promised thee. Lay it to thy heart, and farewell.'
Glamis thou art, and Cawdor; and shalt be
What thou art promised. Yet do I fear thy
   nature:
It is too full o'the milk of human kindness,
To catch the nearest way. Hie thee hither,
That I may pour my spirits in thine ear,
And chastise with the valour of my tongue
All that impedes thee from the golden round,
Which fate and metaphysical aid doth seem
To have thee crowned withal.
(*Enter* 1ST MESSENGER.)
What is your tidings?
MESSENGER: The king comes here tonight.
LADY MACBETH: Thou'rt mad to say it!
Is not thy master with him?
MESSENGER: Our Thane is coming;
One of my fellows had the speed of him.
LADY MACBETH: He brings great news.
(*Exit* 1ST MESSENGER.)
The raven himself is hoarse
That croaks the fatal entrance of Duncan
Under my battlements. Come, you spirits

C

That tend on mortal thoughts, unsex me here
And fill me, from the crown to the toe, top-full
Of direst cruelty.
(*Enter* MACBETH.)
Great Glamis, worthy Cawdor!
Greater than both by the all-hail hereafter!
(*They embrace.*)

MACBETH: Duncan comes here tonight.

LADY MACBETH: And when goes hence?

MACBETH: Tomorrow, as he purposes.

LADY MACBETH: O never
Shall sun that morrow see! Look like the
    innocent flower,
But be the serpent under't.
(*Voices heard off-stage.*)
He that's coming
Must be provided for—

MACBETH: We will speak further. (*He goes to door stage right.*)
(DUNCAN *is approaching, accompanied by* BANQUO *and* ROSS.)

DUNCAN: This castle hath a pleasant seat; the air
Nimbly and sweetly recommends itself
Unto our gentle senses.
(LADY MACBETH *goes to meet him.*)
See, see, our honoured hostess—
(LADY MACBETH *gives a curtsey.*)
Where's the Thane of Cawdor?

MACBETH: (*Re-entering from door threshold.*) Your servant.
(MACBETH *steps forward and bows.*)

DUNCAN: (*To* LADY MACBETH.) Fair and noble hostess, we
are your guest tonight.
Give me your hand.
(LADY MACBETH *leads him out followed by* ROSS *and* BANQUO. MACBETH *remains.*)

MACBETH: If it were done, when 'tis done, then 'twere well
It were done quickly. He's here in double trust:
First, as I am his kinsman and his subject,

Strong both against the deed; then, as his host,
Who should against his murderer shut the door,
Not bear the knife myself. I have no spur
To prick the sides of my intent, but only
Vaulting ambition, which o'erleaps itself
And falls on the other.
(*Enter* LADY MACBETH.)
How now? What news? Hath he asked for me?

LADY MACBETH: Know you not he has?

MACBETH: We will proceed no further in this business.

LADY MACBETH: And live a coward in thine own esteem,
Letting 'I dare not' wait upon 'I would',
Like the poor cat i' the adage?
But screw your courage to the sticking place,
And we'll not fail. When Duncan is asleep—
What cannot you and I perform upon
The unguarded Duncan?
(BANQUO *is approaching.*)

MACBETH: (*Off-stage*) Who's there?
MACBETH *goes to meet him at window,* LADY
MACBETH *behind.*)

BANQUO: (*From window.*) A friend.
What, sir, not yet at rest? The King's a-bed.
I dreamt last night of the three sisters.
To you they have showed some truth.

MACBETH: I think not of them. Good repose the while.

BANQUO: Thanks, sir; the like to you.
(MACBETH *closes shutters.*)

MACBETH: Is this a dagger which I see before me,
The handle toward my hand? Come, let me
clutch thee—
I have thee not and yet I see thee still!
(*A bell sounds.*)
I go, and it is done; the bell invites me.
Hear it not, Duncan, for it is a knell
That summons thee to heaven or to hell.
(*Exit* MACBETH. *Sounds of owls and crickets. Enter*
LADY MACBETH *holding a goblet.*)

LADY MACBETH: That which hath made them drunk hath made
me bold;
The doors are open, and the surfeited grooms
Do mock their charge with snores; I have
drugged their possets.
(*Owl and crickets.*)
I laid their daggers ready.
Had he not resembled
My father as he slept, I had done't.
(*Enter* MACBETH *carrying two blood-stained*
daggers.)
My husband!

MACBETH: I have done the deed. Didst thou not hear a
noise?

LADY MACBETH: I heard the owl scream and the crickets cry.
(*A police siren is heard approaching the house.*
During the following dialogue the car arrives and
the car doors are heard to slam.)

MACBETH: There's one did laugh in 's sleep, and one cried
'Murder!'
One cried 'God bless us!' and 'Amen' the other,
(*Siren stops.*)
As they had seen me with these hangman's hands.

LADY MACBETH: Consider it not so deeply.
These deeds must not be thought
After these ways; so, it will make us mad.

MACBETH: Methought I heard a voice cry, 'Sleep no more!
Macbeth does murder sleep'—
(*Sharp rapping.*)
Whence is that knocking?
(*Sharp rapping.*)
How is't with me when every noise appals me?

LADY MACBETH: My hands are of your colour; but I shame
To wear a heart so white.
Retire we to our chamber.

MACBETH: Wake Duncan with thy knocking! (*Sharp*
rapping.)
I would thou couldst!

(*They leave. The knocking off-stage continues. A door, off-stage, opens and closes. The door into the room opens and the* INSPECTOR *enters an empty room. He seems surprised to find himself where he is. He affects a sarcastic politeness.*)

INSPECTOR: Oh—I'm sorry—is this the National Theatre?

(*A woman, the* HOSTESS, *approaches through the audience.*)

HOSTESS: No.

INSPECTOR: It isn't? Wait a minute—I could have made a mistake . . . is it the National Academy of Dramatic Art, or, as we say down Mexico way, NADA? . . . No? I'm utterly nonplussed. I must have got my wires crossed somewhere. (*He is wandering around the room, looking at the walls and ceiling.*)

Testing, testing—one, two, three . . .

(*To the ceiling. In other words the room is bugged for sound.*)

Is it the home of the Bohemian Light Opera?

HOSTESS: It's *my* home.

INSPECTOR: (*Surprised*) You live here?

HOSTESS: Yes.

INSPECTOR: Don't you find it rather inconvenient, having a lot of preening exhibitionists projecting their voices around the place?—and that's just the audience. I mean, who wants to be packed out night after night by a crowd of fashionable bronchitics saying 'I don't think it's as good as his last one,' and expecting to use your lavatory at will? Not to mention putting yourself at the mercy of any Tom, Dick or Bertolt who can't universalize our predicament without playing ducks and drakes with your furniture arrangements. I don't know why you put up with it. You've got your rights. (*Nosing around he picks up a tea-cosy to reveal a telephone.*) You've even got a telephone. I can see you're not at the bottom of the social heap. What do you do?

HOSTESS: I'm an artist.

INSPECTOR: (*Cheerfully*) Well it's not the first time I've been wrong. Is this 'phone practical?

(*To ceiling again.*) Six seven eight one double one. (*He replaces the receiver.*)

Yes, if you had any pride in your home you wouldn't take

53

standing-room only in your sitting-room lying down.

(*The telephone rings in his hand. He lifts it up.*)

Six seven eight one double one? Clear as a bell. Who do you
want?

(*He looks round.*)

Is Roger here?

(*Into the 'phone.*)

Roger who? Roger and out?

(*He removes the 'phone from his ear and frowns at it.*)

Didn't even say goodbye. Whatever happened to the
tradition of old-world courtesy in this country?

(*He puts the 'phone down just as* 'MACBETH' *and* 'LADY
MACBETH' *re-enter the room.*)

Who are you, pig-face?

'MACBETH': Landovsky.

INSPECTOR: The actor?

'MACBETH': The floor-cleaner in a boiler factory.

INSPECTOR: That's him. I'm a great admirer of yours, you know.
I've followed your career for years.

'MACBETH': I haven't worked for years.

INSPECTOR: What are you talking about?—I saw you last season—
my wife was with me . . .

'MACBETH': It couldn't have been me.

INSPECTOR: It *was* you—you looked great—sounded great—
where were you last year?

'MACBETH': I was selling papers in—

INSPECTOR: (*Triumphantly*)—the newspaper kiosk at the tram
terminus, and you were wonderful! I said to my wife, that's
Landovsky—the actor—isn't he great?! What a character!
Wonderful voice! "Getcha paper!"—up from here (*He
thumps his chest.*)—no strain, every syllable given its value
. . . Well, well, well, so now you're sweeping floors, eh? I
remember you from way back. I remember you when you
were a night-watchman in the builder's yard, and before
that when you were the trolley porter at the mortuary, and
before *that* when you were the button-moulder in *Peer
Gynt* . . . Actually, Pavel, you've had a funny sort of career
—it's not my business, of course, but . . . do you know

54

what you want? It's my opinion that the public is utterly
confused about your intentions. Is this where you saw it all
leading to when you started off so bravely all those years
ago? I remember you in your first job. You were a messenger
—post office, was it . . .?

'MACBETH': *Antony and Cleopatra.*

INSPECTOR: Right!—You see—I'm utterly confused myself. Tell
me Pavel, why did you give it all up? You were a star! I saw
your Hamlet, your Stanley Kowolski—I saw your Romeo
with what's her name—wonderful girl, whatever happened
to *her?* Oh my God, don't tell me!—could I have your
autograph, it's not for me, it's for my daughter—

'LADY MACBETH': I'd rather not—the last time I signed something
I didn't work for two years.

INSPECTOR: Now, look, don't blame *us* if the parts just stopped
coming. Maybe you got over-exposed.

'LADY MACBETH': I was working in a restaurant at the time.

INSPECTOR: (*Imperturbably*) There you are, you see. The public's
very funny about that sort of thing. They don't want to get
dressed up and arrange a baby-sitter only to find that they've
paid good money to see *Hedda Gabler* done by a waitress.
I'm beginning to understand why your audience is confined
to your circle of acquaintances. (*To audience.*) Don't move.
I mean, it gives one pause, doesn't it? 'Tonight Macbeth
will be played by Mr Landovsky who last season scored a
personal success in the newspaper kiosk at the tram terminus
and has recently been seen washing the floors in number
three boiler factory. The role of Lady Macbeth is in the
capable hands of Vera from The Dirty Spoon' . . . It sounds
like a rough night.

(*The words 'rough night' operate as a cue for the entrance of the
actor playing* MACDUFF.

Enter MACDUFF.)

MACDUFF: O horror, horror, horror!
    Confusion now hath made his masterpiece!

INSPECTOR: What's *your* problem, sunshine? Don't tell me you've
found a corpse—I come here to be taken out of myself, not
to be shown a reflection of the banality of my own life. Why

55

don't you go out and come in again. I'll get out of the way. Is this seat taken?

HOSTESS: I'm afraid the performance is not open to the public.

(*Enter* 'ROSS', 'BANQUO', 'MALCOLM', *but not acting.*)

INSPECTOR: I should hope not indeed. That would be acting without authority—acting without authority!—you'd never believe I make it up as I go along . . . Right!—sorry to have interrupted.

(*He sits down. Pause.*)

Any time you're ready.

(*The* HOSTESS *retires. The* ACTORS *remain standing on the stage, unco-operative, taking their lead from* 'MACBETH'. *The* INSPECTOR *leaves his seat and approaches* 'MACBETH'.)

INSPECTOR: (*To* 'MACBETH'.) Now listen, you stupid bastard, you'd better get rid of the idea that there's a special *Macbeth* which you do when I'm not around, and some other *Macbeth* for when I *am* around which isn't worth doing. You've only got one *Macbeth*. Because I'm giving this party and there ain't no other. It's what we call a one-party system. I'm the cream in your coffee, the sugar in your tank, and the breeze blowing down your neck. So let's have a little of the old trouper spirit, because if I walk out of this show I take it with me.

(*He goes back to his seat and says genially to audience.*)

So sorry to interrupt.

(*He sits down.* 'MACBETH' *is still unco-operative.* 'ROSS' *takes the initiative. He talks quietly to* 'BANQUO', *who leaves to make his entrance again.* 'LADY MACBETH' *goes behind screen stage left.*)

ROSS: Goes the King hence today?

(*Pause*)

MACBETH: He does; he did appoint so.

(*The acting is quick and casual.*)

ROSS: The night has been unruly.

MACBETH: 'Twas a rough night.

(MACDUFF *enters as before.*)

MACDUFF: O horror, horror, horror!

Confusion now hath made his masterpiece.

Most sacrilegious murder hath broke ope
The Lord's anointed temple and stole thence
The life of the building.

MACBETH: What is't you say? The life? Mean you His
Majesty?

BANQUO: Ring the alarum bell. Murder and treason.

LADY MACBETH: What's the business,
Speak, speak!

MACDUFF: O gentle lady,
'Tis not for you to hear what I can speak.
(*Alarum bell sounds.*)
Our royal master's murdered.

LADY MACBETH: Woe, alas! What, in our house!

ROSS: Too cruel, anywhere.

MACBETH: (*Enters with bloody daggers.*) Had I but died an
hour before this chance
I had lived a blessed time; far from this instant
There's nothing serious in mortality.
All is but toys; renown and grace is dead,
The wine of life is drawn, and the mere lees
Is left this vault to brag of.
(*Enter MALCOLM.*)

MALCOLM: What is amiss?

MACBETH: You are, and do not know't.

MACDUFF: Your royal father's murdered.

MALCOLM: By whom?

MACBETH: Those of his chamber, as it seemed, had done 't:
Their hands and faces were all badged with
blood:
So were these daggers which unwip't we found
upon their pillows;
Oh yet I do repent me of my fury
That I did kill them.

MALCOLM: Wherefore did you so?

LADY MACBETH: (*Swooning*) Help me hence, ho!

MACBETH: Look to the lady!

MACDUFF: Look to the lady!
(LADY MACBETH *is being taken out.*)

MACBETH: Let us briefly put on manly readiness
And meet in the hall together.
(*All, except* MALCOLM *exeunt.*)

MALCOLM: (*Aside*) To show an unfelt sorrow is an office
Which the false man does easy. I'll to England.
This murderous shaft that's shot
Hath not yet lighted; and our safest way
Is to avoid the aim. Therefore to horse.
(*Exit.*)

MACDUFF: Malcolm and Donalbain, the King's two sons,
Are stolen away and fled, which puts upon them
Suspicion of the deed.

ROSS: Then 'tis most like
The sovereignty will fall upon Macbeth?

MACDUFF: He is already named and gone to Scone
To be invested.
(*Fanfare.*
They leave the stage. MACBETH *in cloak crowns
himself standing above screen.*
The INSPECTOR *applauds and steps forward into the
light.*)

INSPECTOR: Very good. Very good! And so nice to have a play
with a happy ending for a change.
(*Other* ACTORS *come on-stage in general light.*)
(*To* LADY MACBETH.) Darling, you were marvellous.

'LADY MACBETH': I'm not your darling.

INSPECTOR: I know, and you weren't marvellous either, but when
in Rome *parlezvous* as the natives do. Actually, I thought
you were better on the radio.

'LADY MACBETH': I haven't been on radio.

INSPECTOR: You've been on mine.
(*To the general audience the* INSPECTOR *says.*)
Please don't leave the building. You may use the lavatory
but leave the door open.
(*To* MACBETH.)
Stunning! Incredible! Absolutely fair to middling.

'MACBETH': You were rubbish!

INSPECTOR: Look, just because I didn't laugh out loud it doesn't

58

mean I wasn't enjoying it. (*To* HOSTESS.) Which one were
you?

HOSTESS: I'm not in it.

INSPECTOR: You're in it, up to here. It's pretty clear to me that
this flat is being used for entertaining men. There is a law
about that, you know.

HOSTESS: I don't think *Macbeth* is what was meant.

INSPECTOR: Who's to say what was meant? Words can be your
friend or your enemy, depending on who's throwing the
book, so watch your language. (*He passes a finger over the
furniture.*) Look at this! Filthy! If this isn't a disorderly
house I've never seen one, and I have seen one. I've had
this place watched you know.

HOSTESS: I know.

INSPECTOR: Gave themselves away, did they?

HOSTESS: It was the uniforms mainly, and standing each side of
the door.

INSPECTOR: My little team. Boris and Maurice.

HOSTESS: One of them examined everyone's papers and the other
one took down the names.

INSPECTOR: Yes, one of them can read and the other one can
write. That's why we go around in threes—I have to keep
an eye on those bloody intellectuals.

'MACDUFF': Look, what the hell do you want?

INSPECTOR: I want to know who's in tonight.

(*He looks at a list of names in his notebook and glances over
the audience.*)

HOSTESS: They are all personal friends of mine.

INSPECTOR: Now let's see who we've got here. (*Looking at the
list.*) Three stokers, two labourers, a van-driver's mate,
janitors, street cleaners, a jobbing gardener, painter and
decorator, chambermaid, two waiters, farmhand. . . . You
seem to have cracked the problem of the working-class
audience. If there isn't a catch I'll put you up as a heroine
of the revolution. I mean, the counter-revolution. No, I tell
a lie, I mean the normalization—Yes, I know. Who is that
horny-handed son of the soil?

(*The* INSPECTOR *points his torch at different people in the audience.*)

HOSTESS: (*Looking into the audience.*) Medieval historian . . .
professor of philosophy . . . painter . . .

INSPECTOR: And decorator?

HOSTESS: No . . . lecturer . . . student . . . student . . . defence
lawyer . . . Minister of Health in the caretaker government . . .

INSPECTOR: What's he doing now?

HOSTESS: He's a caretaker.

INSPECTOR: Yes, well, I must say a column of tanks is a great
leveller. How about the defence lawyer?

HOSTESS: He's sweeping the streets now.

INSPECTOR: You see, some went down, but some went up. Fair
do's. Well, I'll tell you what. I don't want to spend all day
taking statements. It's frankly not worth the candle for three
years' maximum and I know you've been having a run of
bad luck all round—jobs lost, children failing exams, letters
undelivered, driving licences withdrawn, passports
indefinitely postponed—and nothing on paper. It's as if the
system had a mind of its own; so why don't you give it a
chance, and I'll give you one. I'm really glad I caught you
before you closed. If I can make just one tiny criticism . . .
Shakespeare—or the Old Bill, as we call him in the force—
is not a popular choice with my chief, owing to his
popularity with the public, or, as we call it in the force, the
filth. The fact is, when you get a universal and timeless
writer like Shakespeare, there's a strong feeling that he could
be spitting in the eyes of the beholder when he should be
keeping his mind on Verona—hanging around the 'gents'.
You know what I mean? Unwittingly, of course. He didn't
know he was doing it, at least you couldn't prove he did,
which is what makes the chief so prejudiced against him.
The chief says he'd rather you stood up and said, 'There is
no freedom in this country', then there's nothing underhand
and we all know where we stand. You get your lads together
and we get our lads together and when it's all over, one of
us is in power and you're in gaol. That's freedom in action.
But what we don't like is a lot of people being cheeky and
saying they are only Julius Caesar or Coriolanus or Macbeth.

60

Otherwise we are going to start treating them the same as the ones who say they are Napoleon. Got it?

'MACBETH': We obey the law and we ask no more of you.

INSPECTOR: The law? I've got the Penal Code tattooed on my whistle, Landovsky, and there's a lot about you in it. Section 98, subversion—anyone acting out of hostility to the state . . . Section 100, incitement—anyone acting out of hostility to the state . . . I could nick you just for acting— and the sentence is double for an organized group, which I can make stick on Robinson Crusoe and his man any day of the week. So don't tell me about the laws.

'MACBETH': We're protected by the Constitution . . .

INSPECTOR: Dear God, and we call you intellectuals. Personally I can't read that stuff. Nobody talks like that so it's not reasonable to expect them to live like it. The way I see it, life is lived off the record. It's altogether too human for the written word, it happens in pictures . . . metaphors . . . A few years ago you suddenly had it on toast, but when they gave you an inch you overplayed your hand and rocked the boat so they pulled the rug from under you, and now you're in the doghouse . . . I mean, that is pure fact. Metaphorically speaking. It describes what happened to you in a way that anybody can understand.

(BANQUO, *henceforth* CAHOOT, *howls like a dog, barks, falls silent on his hands and knees.*)

INSPECTOR: Sit! Here, boy! What's his name?

'MACBETH': Cahoot.

INSPECTOR: The social parasite and slanderer of the state?

CAHOOT: The writer.

INSPECTOR: That's him. You're a great favourite down at the nick, you know. We're thinking of making you writer in residence for a couple of years; four if you're a member of a recognized school, which I can make stick on a chimpanzee with a box of alphabet bricks. (*Smiles*) Would you care to make a statement?

CAHOOT: 'Thou hast it now: King, Cawdor, Glamis, all
    As the weird sisters promised . . .'

INSPECTOR: Kindly leave my wife's family out of this.

CAHOOT: '. . . and I fear
        thou playedst most foully for't . . .'
INSPECTOR: Foul . . . fair . . . which is which? That's two witches:
        one more and we can do the show right here.
CAHOOT: '. . . Yet it was said
        It should not stand in thy posterity . . .'
INSPECTOR: If you think you can drive a horse and cart through
        the law of slander by quoting blank verse at me, Cahoot,
        you're going to run up against what we call poetic justice:
        which means we get you into line if we have to chop one of
        your feet off. You know as well as I do that this performance
        of yours goes right against the spirit of normalization. When
        you clean out the stables, Cahoot, the muck is supposed to
        go into the gutter, not find its way back into the stalls. (*To*
        ALL *generally*.) I blame sport and religion for all this, you
        know. An Olympic games here, a papal visit there, and
        suddenly you think you can take liberties with your freedom
        . . . amateur theatricals, organized groups, committees of all
        kinds—listen, I've arrested more committees (*to* 'BANQUO')
        than you've had dog's dinners. I arrested the Committee to
        Defend the Unjustly Persecuted for saying I unjustly
        persecuted the Committee for Free Expression, which I
        arrested for saying there wasn't any—so if I find that this
        is a benefit for the Canine Defence League you're going to
        feel my hand on your collar and I don't care if Moscow
        Dynamo is at home to the Vatican in the European Cup.
        ('BANQUO' *growls*.)
        What is the matter with him?
'MACBETH': He's been made a non-person.
INSPECTOR: Has he? Well, between you and me and these three
        walls and especially the ceiling, barking up the wrong tree
        comes under anti-state agitation. I'm not having him fouling
        the system let alone the pavements just because he's got an
        identity crisis.
'MACBETH': Your system could do with a few antibodies. If
        you're afraid to risk the infection of an uncontrolled idea,
        the first time a new one gets in, it'll run through your
        system like a rogue bacillus. Remember the last time.
62

INSPECTOR: (*Pause.*) Yes. Well, a lot of water has passed through the Penal Code since then. Things are normalizing nicely. I expect this place will be back to normal in five minutes . . . Eh? Nice Dog! Well, I wonder what the weather's like outside . . . (*Moves*) Please leave in an orderly manner, and don't cheek the policeman on the way out.

(*'Phone rings. He picks it up . . . listens, replaces it.*)

Cloudy, with a hint of rain.

(*He exits.*

He leaves. The police car is heard to depart with its siren going.)

CAHOOT: Let it come down!

(*The performance continues from Act Three Scene One. All exeunt except* CAHOOT.)

BANQUO: Thou has it now: King, Cawdor, Glamis, all
As the weird women promised; and I fear
Thou playdst most foully for't. Yet it was said
It should not stand in thy posterity
But that myself should be the root and father
Of many kings. If there come truth from them,
As upon thee, Macbeth, their speeches shine,
Why by the verities on thee made good
(MACBETH *enters.*)
May they not be my oracles as well
And set me up in hope? But hush! No more.

MACBETH: Tonight we hold a solemn supper, sir,
And I'll request your presence.
Ride you this afternoon?

BANQUO: Ay, my good lord.

MACBETH: Fail not our feast.

BANQUO: My lord, I will not.
(*Exit* BANQUO.)

MACBETH: Our fears in Banquo
Stick deep; and in his royalty of nature
Reigns that which would be feared. He chid the sisters
When first they put the name of king upon me,
And bade them speak to him. Then, prophet-like

63

They hailed him father to a line of kings.
Upon my head they placed a fruitless crown
And put a barren sceptre in my grip,
Thence to be wrenched with an unlineal hand,
No son of mine succeeding. If it be so,
For Banquo's issue have I filed my mind,
For them the gracious Duncan have I murdered.
Rather than so, come, fate, into the list
And champion me to the utterance!
(MACBETH *moves screen to reveal two* MURDERERS.)
Was it not yesterday we spoke together?
(*Lights down.*)

1ST MURDERER: It was, so please your highness.

MACBETH: Well then now,
Have you considered of my speeches? Know
That it was he in the times past which held you
So under fortune, which you thought had been
Our innocent self.

1ST MURDERER: You made it known to us.

MACBETH: I did so. Are you so gospelled,
To pray for this good man and for his issue,
Whose heavy hand hath bowed you to the grave,
And beggared yours for ever?

2ND MURDERER: I am one, my liege,
Whom the vile blows and buffets of the world
Hath so incensed that I am reckless what I do
To spite the world.

1ST MURDERER: And I another,
So weary with disasters, tugged with fortune,
That I would set my life on any chance
To mend it or be rid on't.

MACBETH: Both of you
Know Banquo was your enemy.

MURDERERS: True, my lord.

MACBETH: So is he mine, and though I could
With bare-faced power sweep him from my sight
And bid my will avouch it, yet I must not.

2ND MURDERER: We shall, my lord

Perform what you command us.

1ST MURDERER: We are resolved, my lord.

(EASY's *lorry has been heard to draw up outside.*
The MURDERERS *go to the window and open*
shutters. MACBETH *leaves saying.*)

MACBETH: (*Aside*) It is concluded! Banquo, thy soul's flight,
If it find heaven, must find it out tonight.

(*The* MURDERERS *take up position to ambush*
BANQUO. EASY *appears at window and says.*)

EASY: Buxtons . . . Almost Leamington Spa.

(*The* MURDERERS *are surprised to see him.* EASY
disappears from window: they peer outside to see
him, but meanwhile EASY *has entered room.*)
Cakehops.

1ST MURDERER: But who did bid thee join with us?

EASY: Buxtons.

(*Pause*)

2ND MURDERER: (*With misgiving.*) He needs not our mistrust,
since he delivers
Our offices and what we have to do
To the direction just.

EASY: Eh?

1ST MURDERER: Then stand with us;
The west yet glimmers with some streaks of day.
Now spurs the lated traveller apace
To gain the timely inn; and near approaches
The subject of our watch.

(*Pause*)

EASY: Eh?

BANQUO: (*Off-stage*) Give us a light, here, ho!

2ND MURDERER: Then 'tis he.

(*Enter* BANQUO *in window.*)

1ST MURDERER: Stand to 't!

BANQUO: It will be rain tonight.

1ST MURDERER: Let it come down!

(*The two* MURDERERS *attack* BANQUO.)

BANQUO: O treachery!

(*He flees off-stage with the two* MURDERERS *in*

pursuit. EASY *remains, looking bewildered. The* HOSTESS *appears from the audience again.*)

EASY: Buxtons . . . cake hops . . . almost Leamington Spa . . .

(*The* HOSTESS *leads him off-stage. Light and music for* MACBETH'*s feast.* MACBETH *enters with* LADY MACBETH *and guests in attendance.*)

MACBETH: You know your own degrees, sit down.
At first and last a hearty welcome.

GUESTS: Thanks to your majesty.

MACBETH: Ourself will mingle with society
And play the humble host.

(*The* GUESTS *have brought their own stools and goblets.* LADY MACBETH *enters likewise.* 1ST MURDERER *enters with* EASY, *remaining at the edge of the stage.*)

Be large in mirth. Anon we'll drink a measure
The table round.

(*He sees* 1ST MURDERER *and goes to him.*)

There's blood upon thy face!

1ST MURDERER: 'Tis Banquo's then.

MACBETH: Is he dispatched?

1ST MURDERER: My lord, his throat is cut;
That I did for him.

MACBETH: Thanks for that.
Get thee gone! Tomorrow we will hear ourselves again.

(*Exit* MURDERER, *followed by* EASY. *During the scene* EASY *is hovering at the fringes, hoping to catch someone's eye. His entrances and exits coincide with those for* BANQUO'*s* GHOST, *who is invisible, and he only appears in* MACBETH'*s eyeline.* MACBETH *does his best to ignore him.*)

LADY MACBETH: My royal lord,
You do not give the cheer.

MACBETH: Sweet remembrancer!
Now good digestion wait on appetite,
And health on both!

ROSS: May't please your highness sit.

MACBETH: Here had we now our country's honour roofed,
Were the graced person of our Banquo present.

ROSS: His absence, sir,
Lays blame upon his promise. Please't your highness
To grace us with your royal company?
Here is a place reserved.
(*EASY enters at door stage right.*)

MACBETH: Where?

ROSS: Here, my good lord. What is't that moves your highness?

MACBETH: Which of you have done this?

ROSS: What, my good lord?

MACBETH: Thou canst not say I did it; never shake
Thy gory locks at me.

ROSS: Gentlemen, rise. His highness is not well.

LADY MACBETH: Sit, worthy friends. My lord is often thus;
The fit is momentary; upon a thought
He will again be well.
(*She crosses to MACBETH.*)
Are you a man?

MACBETH: Ay, and a bold one, that dare look on that
Which might appall the devil.

LADY MACBETH: O proper stuff!
Why do you make such faces? When all's done
You look but on a stool.
(*EASY appears at window.*)

MACBETH: Prithee, see there!
Behold! Look! Lo!
(*He points, but EASY has lost his nerve, and
disappears just as she turns round.*)

LADY MACBETH: What, quite unmanned in folly?

MACBETH: If I stand here, I saw him. This is more strange
Than such a murder is.

LADY MACBETH: My worthy lord,
Your noble friends do lack you.

MACBETH: I do forget.

(*He recovers somewhat.*)

Do not muse at me, my most worthy friends:
I have a strange infirmity, which is nothing
To those that know me. Come love and health to
    all!
Then I'll sit down. Give me some wine; Fill full!
I drink to the general joy o' the whole table,
And to our dear friend Banquo, whom we miss.
Would he were here! To all—and him—we thirst,
And all to all.

GUESTS: Our duties and the pledge!

(*However,* EASY *tries again, reappearing in*
MACBETH'*s sight above screen stage right.*)

MACBETH: Avaunt, and quit my sight!

(EASY *quits his sight.*)

Let the earth hide thee!
Thy bones are marrowless, thy blood is cold.

LADY MACBETH: Think of this, good peers,
But as a thing of custom; 'tis no other;
Only it spoils the pleasure of the time.

(EASY *appears at the window again.*)

MACBETH: Hence, horrible shadow!
Unreal mockery, hence!

(*He closes shutters. He recovers again.*)

Why, so; being gone,
I am a man again. Pray you sit still.

LADY MACBETH: (*Aside to* MACBETH.) You have displaced the
    mirth, broke the good meeting
With most admired disorder.

(*To the* GUESTS.) At once, good night.
Stand not upon the order of your going;
But go at once.

(*The* GUESTS *rise and depart.*)

ROSS: Good night; and better health
Attend his majesty!

LADY MACBETH: A kind good-night to all!

(*Lights down.*)

MACBETH: It will have blood, they say; blood will have blood.

68

Stones have been known to move and trees to
    speak;
And betimes I will—to the weird sisters.
More shall they speak; for now I am bent to
    know
By the worst means the worst.
(*Thunder and lightning. Three* WITCHES.)

WITCHES: Double, double, toil and trouble;
    Fire burn, and cauldron bubble.

1ST WITCH: By the pricking of my thumbs,
    Something wicked this way comes.
    (*Enter* MACBETH.)

MACBETH: How now, you secret, black, and midnight hags!
    What is't you do?

WITCHES: A deed without a name.

MACBETH: I conjure you, by that which you profess,
    Howe'er you come to know it, answer me—

1ST WITCH: Say if thou'dst rather hear it from our mouths
    Or from our masters.

MACBETH: Call 'em. Let me see 'em.
    (*The 'Apparitions' of Shakespeare's play are here*
    translated into voices, amplified and coming from
    different parts of the auditorium. Evidently
    MACBETH *can see the 'Apparition' from which*
    each voice comes. Thunder.)

1ST VOICE: Macbeth, Macbeth, Macbeth, beware Macduff!
    Beware the Thane of Fife! Dismiss me. Enough.

MACBETH: Whate'er thou art, for thy good caution, thanks;
    Thou hast harped my fear aright.

2ND VOICE: Macbeth, Macbeth, Macbeth!

MACBETH: Had I three ears, I'd hear thee.

2ND VOICE: Be bloody, bold, and resolute; laugh to scorn
    The power of man; for none of woman born
    Shall harm Macbeth.

MACBETH: Then live Macduff; What need I fear of thee?
    (*Thunder.*
    Exit WITCHES.)
    What is this

That rises like the issue of a king,
And wears upon his baby brow the round
And top of a sovereignty?

CHILD'S VOICE: Be lion-mettled, proud, and take no care
Who chafes, who frets, or where conspirers are;
Macbeth shall never vanquished be, until
Great Birnam Wood to high Dunsinane Hill
Shall come against him.

MACBETH: That will never be.
Who can impress the forest, bid the tree
Unfix his earth-bound root? Yet my heart
Throbs to know one thing:

WITCHES: (*Off-stage*) Seek to know no more.
Show his eyes and grieve his heart;
Come like shadows, so depart.

MACBETH: Where are they? Gone! Let this pernicious hour
Stand aye accursed in the calendar.
Come in, without there.
(*Enter* LENNOX.)

LENNOX: What is your grace's will.

MACBETH: Saw you the weird sisters?

LENNOX: No my lord.
(EASY *passes window.*)

MACBETH: Who was't come by?

LENNOX: 'Tis two or three my lord, that bring you word
that
Macduff's fled to England.

MACBETH: Fled to England?
(EASY *enters timidly.*)

EASY: Useless . . . useless . . . Buxtons cake hops . . . artichoke
almost Leamington Spa . . . [*Afternoon . . . afternoon . . .
Buxtons blocks and that . . . lorry from Leamington Spa.]

'MACBETH': What?
(*General light.* OTHERS, *but not* MALCOLM *or* MACDUFF,
approach out of curiosity. 'MACBETH' *says to* HOSTESS.)
Who the hell is this man?

HOSTESS: (*To* EASY.) Who are you?
(EASY *has his clipboard which he offers.*)

EASY: Buxton cake hops.

HOSTESS: Don't sign anything.

EASY: Blankets up middling if season stuck, after plug-holes kettle-drummed lightly A412 mildly Rickmansworth—clipped awful this water ice, zig-zaggled—splash quarterly trainers as Micky Mouse snuffle—cup—evidently knick-knacks quarantine only if bacteriologic waistcoats crumble pipe—sniffle then postbox but shazam!!!! Even platforms—dandy avuncular Donald Duck never-the-less minty magazines! [*Translation—see page 20]

(*Pause*)

'MACBETH': Eh?

(EASY *produces a phrase book and starts thumbing through it.*)

EASY: (*Triumphantly*) Ah!

(*He passes the* HOSTESS *his phrase book, indicating what she should read. She examines the page.*)

HOSTESS: He says his postillion has been struck by lightning.

EASY: Hat rack timble cuckoo pig exit dunce!

'MACBETH': What?

EASY: Dunce!

'MACBETH': What?

EASY: Cuckoo pig exit what.

(*Nodding agreeably.*) Cake hops properly Buxtons.

(*The* HOSTESS *flips through the book.*)

HOSTESS: Cake hops.

EASY: Cake hops.

HOSTESS: Timber or wood.

EASY: Timber or wood—properly Buxtons.

HOSTESS: I'm so sorry about this . . .

EASY: Right. Timber or wood—properly Buxtons. I'm so sorry about this.

(*He opens shutters to reveal his lorry.*)

Ankle so artichoke—almost Leamington Spa.

LENNOX: Oh. He's got a lorry out there.

HOSTESS: Lorry load of wood or timber.

EASY: I'm so sorry about this.

HOSTESS: Don't apologize.

EASY: Don't apologize.

LENNOX: Oh, you do speak the language!

EASY: Oh, you do speak the language.

'MACBETH': No—we speak the language!

EASY: We speak the language.

LENNOX: Cretin is he?

EASY: Pan-stick-trog.

> (*Everybody leaves.*
> *Enter* MALCOLM AND MACDUFF.)

MALCOLM: Let us seek out some desolate shade, and there
Weep our sad bosoms empty.

MACDUFF: Let us rather
Hold fast the mortal sword; and like good men
Bestride our down-fallen birthdom. Each new morn
New widows howl, new orphans cry, new sorrows
Strike heaven on the face, that it resounds
As if it felt with Scotland, and yelled out
Like syllable of dolour.

MALCOLM: This tyrant, whose sole name blisters our tongues,
Was once thought honest.

MACDUFF: Bleed, bleed, poor country!
> (*Police siren is heard in distance.*)

MALCOLM: It weeps, it bleeds, and each new day a gash
Is added to her wounds.

MACDUFF: O Scotland, Scotland!
O nation miserable,
With an untitled tyrant, bloody-sceptred,
When shalt thou see thy wholesome days again.
See who comes here.
> (*Siren stops.*)

MALCOLM: My countryman; but yet I know him not.
> (*The police car has been wailing on its way back.*
> INSPECTOR *enters.*)

MACDUFF: Stands Scotland where it did?

INSPECTOR: Och aye, it's a braw bricht moonlicht nicked, and so are you, you haggis-headed dumbwits, hoots mon ye must think I was born yesterday. (*He drops the accent: to the audience*)—Stay where you are and nobody use the lavatory...

72

(CAHOOT *enters.*)

Cahoots mon! Where's McLandovsky got himself?

(EASY *enters.* HOSTESS *follows.*)

EASY: Useless, git . . . [*Afternoon, sir . . .]

INSPECTOR: Who are you, pig-face?

(INSPECTOR *grabs him.* EASY *yelps and looks at his watch.*)

EASY: Poxy queen! [*Twenty past ouch.]

Marzipan clocks! [*Watch it!]

INSPECTOR: What?

HOSTESS: He doesn't understand you.

INSPECTOR: What's that language he's talking?

HOSTESS: At the moment we're not sure if it's a language or a clinical condition.

EASY: (*Aggrieved*) Quinces carparks! (*Offering the clipboard.*)

Cake-hops—Buxton's almost Leamington Spa.

HOSTESS: He's delivering wood and wants someone to sign for it.

EASY: . . . wood and wants someone to sign for it.

INSPECTOR: Wood?

HOSTESS: He's got a two-ton artichoke out there.

INSPECTOR: What???

HOSTESS: I mean a lorry.

(CAHOOT *taps* EASY *on shoulder.*)

CAHOOT: Useless . . . [*Afternoon . . .]

EASY: (*Absently*) Useless . . . (*then sees who it is.*)

Cahoot! Geraniums!? [*How are you!?]

CAHOOT: Gymshoes. Geraniums? [*Fine. How are you?]

EASY: Gymshoes.

CAHOOT: Upside cakeshops? (*Have you brought the blocks?]

EASY: Slab. [*Yes.]

CAHOOT: Almost Leamington Spa? [*From Leamington Spa?]

EASY: Slab, git. Even artichoke. [*Yes, sir. I've got a lorry.]

CAHOOT: Cube. [*Thanks.]

(*He signs clipboard.*)

EASY: Cube, git. [*Thank you, sir.]

INSPECTOR: Just a minute. What the hell are you talking about?

CAHOOT: Afternoon, squire!

INSPECTOR: Afternoon. Who's your friend?

HOSTESS: He's the cake-hops man.

73

INSPECTOR: Well, why can't he say so?

CAHOOT: He only speaks Dogg.

INSPECTOR: What?

CAHOOT: Dogg.

INSPECTOR: Dogg?

CAHOOT: Haven't you heard of it?

INSPECTOR: Where did you learn it?

CAHOOT: You don't learn it, you catch it.

    (EASY *notices* 'MALCOLM'.)

EASY: Useless. [*Afternoon.]

'MALCOLM': Useless . . . Geraniums?

EASY: Gymshoes. Geraniums?

'MALCOLM': Gymshoes . . . cube . . .

EASY: (*To* CAHOOT.) Blankets up middling if senses stuck, after plug-holes kettle-drummed lightly A412 mildly Rickmansworth.

'MALCOLM': Rickmansworth.

'MACDUFF': (*To* 'MALCOLM', *heading for the door*.) He needs a bit of a hand . . .

EASY: Slab.

'MALCOLM': (*Leaving*.) . . . with the cake-hops . . .

EASY: Clipped awful this water ice zig-zaggled.

CAHOOT: His mate got struck down by lightning.

HOSTESS: Shazam . . .

EASY: Slab.

CAHOOT: (*Hands* EASY *the plans*.) Albatross. [*Plans.]

    (*To* EASY.) Easy! Brick . . .

EASY: Slab, git.

CAHOOT: Brick. (*He positions* EASY *for building steps*.)

EASY: Brick? [*Here?]

CAHOOT: Cake-hops. Brick.

EASY: Cube, git. [*Thanks, sir.]

CAHOOT/HOSTESS: Gymshoes. [*Excellent.]

INSPECTOR: May I remind you we're supposed to be in a period of normalization here.

HOSTESS: Kindly leave the stage. Act Five is about to begin.

INSPECTOR: Is it! I must warn you that anything you say will be taken down and played back at your trial.

HOSTESS: Bicycles! Plank? [*Ready?]
   (*To* INSPECTOR.) Slab. Gymshoes!
   (CAHOOT *and* HOSTESS *leave.*
   INSPECTOR *and* EASY *are left.*)
INSPECTOR: What gymshoes?
EASY: What, git? [*Eleven, sir?]
INSPECTOR: Gymshoes!
EASY: Slab, git.
INSPECTOR: (*Giving up.*) Useless . . .
EASY: (*Enthusiastically*) Useless, git! [*Afternoon, sir!]
INSPECTOR: Right—that's it! (*To ceiling.*) Roger! (*To the audience.*)
   Put your hands on your heads. Put your—placay manos—
   per capita . . . nix toiletto!
   (*'Phone rings.* EASY *answers, hands it to* INSPECTOR.)
EASY: Roger.
INSPECTOR: (*Into 'phone.*) Did you get all that? Clear as a what?
   Acting out of hostility to the Republic. Ten years minimum.
   I want every word in evidence.
   (LADY MACBETH *enters with lighted taper.*)
LADY MACBETH: Hat, daisy puck! Hat, so fie! Sun, dock: hoops
               malign my cattlegrid! Smallish peacocks!
               Flaming scots git, flaming! Fireplace nought
               jammy-flits?
   (*'Phone rings.* INSPECTOR *picks it up.*)
INSPECTOR: (*Into 'phone: pause.*) How the hell do I know? But if
   it's not free expression, I don't know what is!
   (*Hangs up.*)
LADY MACBETH: (*Dry-washing her hands.*) Ash-loving pell-mell on.
               Fairly buses gone Arabia nettle-rash old icicles
               nun. Oh oh oh . . .
               [*Here's the smell of the blood still. All the
               perfumes of Arabia will not sweeten this little
               hand . . .]
   (*She exits.*)
INSPECTOR: (*To* EASY.) She's making it up as she goes along.
   You must think I'm—
   (*But* EASY *is glowing with the light of recognition.*)
EASY: . . . Ah . . . *Macbeth!*

(*Sound of cannon. Smoke.* MACBETH, *armed, appears on battlement.*)

MACBETH: Sack-cloth never pullovers!—wickets to flicks.
Such Birnam cakeshops carousals Dunisnane!
. . . Dovetails oboes Malcolm? Crossly window-
framed!
[*Bring me no more reports. Let them fly all
Till Birnam Wood remove to Dunsinane.
What's the boy Malcolm? Was he not born of
woman?]

(*'Phone rings.* INSPECTOR *snatches it.*)

INSPECTOR: (*Into 'phone.*) What? No—crossly window-framed, I
think . . . Hang about—

MACBETH: Fetlocked his trade-offs cried terrain!
Pram Birnam cakehops bolsters Dunisnane!
[*I will not be afraid of death and bane
Till Birnam Forest come to Dunsinane!]

(*The back of the lorry opens, revealing* MALCOLM *and* OTHERS
within, unloading the blocks etc. INSPECTOR *sees this—speaks
into walkie-talkie.*)

INSPECTOR: Get the chief. Get the chief!

(*One or two—*ROSS, LENNOX—*are to get off the lorry to form a
human chain for the blocks and slabs etc. to pass from*
MACDUFF *in the lorry to* EASY *building the steps.*)

MALCOLM: (*To* MACDUFF *who is in the lorry with him.*)
Jugged cake-hops furnished soon? [*What wood
is this before us?]

INSPECTOR: (*Into walkie-talkie.*) Wilco zebra over!

MACDUFF: Sin cake-hops Birnam, git. [*The woods of
Birnam, sir.]

INSPECTOR: Green Charlie Angels 15 out.

MALCOLM: State level filberts blacken up aglow . . . [*Let
every soldier hew him down a bough . . .]

INSPECTOR: Easy Dogg!

EASY: (*To* INSPECTOR.) Slab, git?

MALCOM: Fry lettuce denial! [*And bear it before him!]

(MACDUFF *and* ANOTHER *leap off lorry; blocks start flowing
towards* EASY, *who builds steps.*

76

LADY MACBETH—*Wails and crys off-stage.*
MESSENGER *enters.*)

MESSENGER: Git! Margarine distract! [*The queen, my lord
is dead!]

MACBETH: Dominoes, et dominoes, et dominoes,
Popsies historical axle-grease, exacts bubbly fins
crock lavender . . .
[*Tomorrow, and tomorrow, and tomorrow,
Creeps in this petty pace from day to day to the
last syllable of recorded time . . .]

INSPECTOR: (*Into 'phone.*) Yes, chief! I think everything's more or
less under control chief . . .
(*This is a lie. The steps are building,* MACBETH *is continuing his
soliloquy, in Dogg: drums and cannons . . . and—*)

MACDUFF: Docket tanks, tarantaras!
[*Make all our trumpets speak!]
(*Trumpets sound.*
And a MESSENGER *rushes in for* MACBETH.)

MESSENGER: Flummoxed git! [*Gracious lord!]

MACBETH: Docket! [*Speak!]

MESSENGER: Cenotaph pay Birnam fry prevailing
cakehops voluntary!
[*As I did stand my watch upon the hill
I looked toward Birnam and anon methought
The wood began to move.]

MACBETH: Quinces icepacks! [*Liar and slave!]
(MESSENGER *retreats.*)
(*Throughout the above,* EASY *is calling for, and receiving, in the
right order, four planks, three slabs, five blocks and nine cubes;
unwittingly using the English words.*
Meanwhile, MACDUFF *has confronted* MACBETH.)

MACDUFF: Spiral, tricycle, spiral! [*Turn, hellhound, turn!]

MACBETH: Rafters Birnam cakehops hobble Dunsinane,
fry counterpane nit crossly window-framed,
fancifully oblong! Sundry cobbles
rattling up so chamberlain. Frantic, Macduff!
Fry butter ban loss underlay—November glove!
[*Though Birnam Wood be come to Dunsinane

> And thou opposed, being of no woman born,
> Yet will I try the last. Before my body
> I throw my warlike shield. Lay on, Macduff;
> and damned be him that first cries 'Hold
> enough!']

INSPECTOR: (*Interrupts.*) All right! That's it!

(*The* INSPECTOR *mounts the now completed platform.*)

INSPECTOR: Thank you. Thank you! Thank you! Scabs!
Stinking slobs—crooks. You're nicked, Jock.
Punks make me puke. Kick back, I'll break necks,
smack chops, put yobs in padlocks and fix facts.
Clamp down on poncy gits like a ton of bricks.
(CAHOOT *applauds.*)

CAHOOT: Gymshoes. Marmalade. Yob?

(*General applause.*)

EASY: Yobbo, git.

INSPECTOR: Boris! Maurice!

(*Two* POLICEMEN *enter and stand to receive slabs thrown to them from the doorway.*)

MACDUFF: Spiral, tricycle, spiral!

INSPECTOR: Slab!

(*Grey slabs are now thrown in and caught by* BORIS *and* MAURICE *who build a wall across the proscenium opening as* MACBETH *and* MACDUFF *fight and* MACBETH *is slain. 'Phone rings.* EASY *picks it up.*)

EASY: Oh, useless gettie!

(*While* EASY *speaks into the 'phone, the* INSPECTOR *directs the building of the wall with the help of* BORIS *and* MAURICE, *the policemen; and* MALCOLM *mounts the platform, taking the crown off the dead* MACBETH, *and finally placing it on his own head.*)

MALCOLM: Nit laughable a cretin awful pig.

EASY: Cretinous fascist pig like one o'clock. Slab?

MALCOLM: Prefer availing avaricious moorhens et factotum after.

EASY: Rozzers. Gendarmes—filth!

MALCOLM: Centre roundabout if partly lawnmowers rosebush.

EASY: Blockhead. Brick as too planks. Slab.

MALCOLM: Gracious laxative. [*Dead butcher.]

EASY: Fishes bastard. Kick his backside so help me Dogg. See if I
     don't. Normalization.

MALCOLM: Vivay hysterical nose poultice.

EASY: Double double toil and trouble.

MALCOLM: Alabaster ominous nifty, blanket noon
         Howl cinder trellis pistols owl by Scone.
         [* So, thanks to all at once and to each one,
         Whom we invite to see us crowned at Scone.]

     (*Fanfare*)

EASY: (*Over fanfare.*) Double double. Double double toil and
     trouble. No. Shakespeare.

     (*Silence*)

     Well, it's been a funny sort of week. But I should be back
     by Tuesday.